The Tryall Lawyer

Leo Bleiman

Copyright © 2024 by Leo Bleiman

Cover Designer: Fiona Suherman

Publishing Assistant: Debbie Oliver

All rights reserved.

No part of this book may be reproduced in any form or by any electronic or mechanical means, including information storage and retrieval systems, without written permission from the author, except for the use of brief quotations in a book review.

For my Family

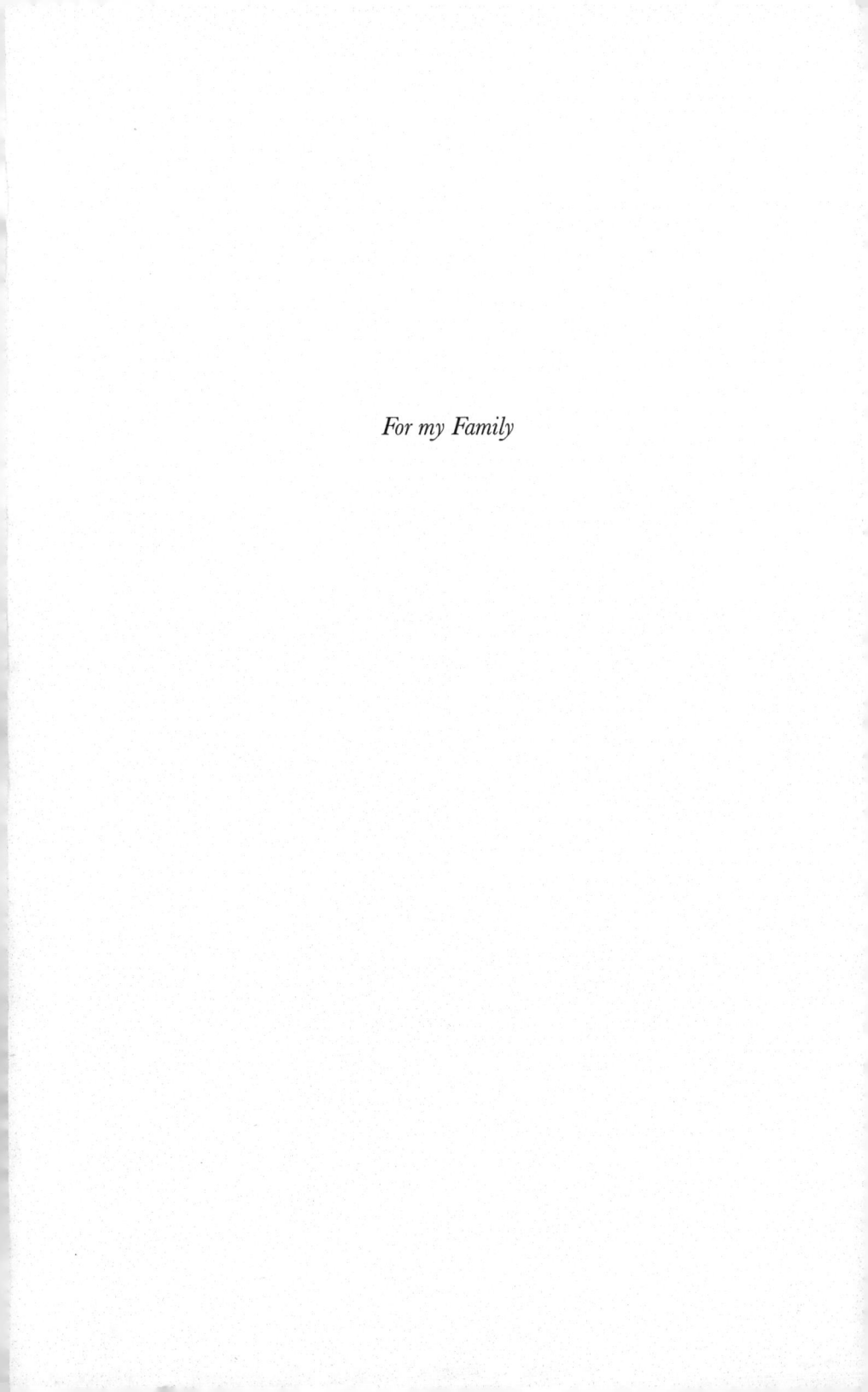

This book is dedicated to the outstanding litigators from both sides of the legal profession who set a high example and inspired me to strive to achieve justice for my clients.

Leo credits the talented, capable, resourceful, intelligent and dedicated assistants with whom he worked over the years, namely, Denise, Sandra, Yolanda, Julie, Elvira, Irma, Susan, Terry, Merry, Monica, Cindy, Laura, and others, who relished the successes, and mourned the losses with him. Without their tireless effort, the practice could not have survived.

He also credits a friend and fellow attorney, Joseph Garofalo, with tremendous support; as well as a longtime friend and children's book author, Susan Wolff, who have endured his tales of the trials and tribulations from the practice of law.

Learn to do right, seek justice, encourage the oppressed, defend the cause of the fatherless, and plead the widow's case. Isaiah 1:17

Contents

Introduction   xiii

Memorable Cases

1. The Law and Me   3
2. The Lottery   11
3. Truth Is Stranger than Fiction: 16
4. Lifesaver   23
5. Time Matters   26
6. Work-Related Baseball Game: 34
7. Call Alarm   43
8. No Grit   46
9. Speeding on the Expressway: 51
10. Teen Shoplifter Suspect: 56
11. Court of Claims   60
12. Cutting Corners   62
13. Missed the Mark   65
14. Missing Humidifier: 68
15. Anti-rotational Braces: 70
16. The Centerline   72
17. Jury Duty   76
18. No Class Action   80
19. Head-On Crash, Smart Jury: 83
20. The Well-Worn Path to Disaster   89
21. Insurance Illusion: 92
22. Handicap Ramp Mishap: 96
23. History Almost Repeats Itself: 99

Memorable Clients

24. Testifying While Intoxicated   105
25. Executive Decisions   109
26. Testifying in Style   112
27. Beyond a Reasonable Doubt   116

28. Patty Melt from Hell	123
29. The Cesspool	126
30. And Four of Those	128
31. Auntie Misbehavin'	131
32. Morning Joe	134
33. Unintended Consequences	138
34. A Tale of Two Hips	142
35. Stick to the Law	144
36. Job Devotion	146
37. Fighting over Doilies	148
38. A Trip to the Dentist	151
39. The Powers of Observation	154
40. A Recipe for Disaster	157
41. Not Mr. Clean	161
42. No Barrel of Fun	163
43. Trial Intangibles	167
44. Credit Card Scam	170
45. Pictures Never Lie?	173
46. Stopping a Bad Guy with a Gun	176

Memorable Clashes

47. No Progress Call	181
48. Please State Your Name	183
49. Motion Call Mayhem	185
50. Local Law	187
51. No Green Card	191
52. Not Guilty—No Divorce	194
53. A Slippery Slope	199
54. Don't Touch Our Sidewalk	202
55. Psycho Arbitrator	206
56. No Good Deed Goes Unpunished	209
57. Contrition	214
58. Contested Divorce	218
59. No Greek Feast	220
60. Money	222
61. The Eye in the Sky	224
62. The Tables Were Turned	228

63. What Happened? 230
64. Safety Last 234
65. Verdict against the Passive Defendant 241
66. No Pain, No Suffering, No Recovery, No Leg 243
67. Hostile Work Environment 246

    Conclusion 249
    About the Author 253

Introduction

This is different from the story of a nationally known and recognized litigator. It reviews cases that form the nuts and bolts of a solo practitioner, often retained based on a contingent fee arrangement. The attorney doesn't charge an hourly rate for his work but must win the cases he handles to be entitled to claim a fee for his services. Some cases settle on a compromise basis. Others must be put before a tribunal to get a result. The decision to proceed with a case is sometimes like rolling the dice at a casino. In the meantime, the costs of moving forward and the time necessarily devoted to pursuing the claims rest with the attorney's talent, creativity, and resourcefulness. These are those stories.

Memorable Cases

THE LAW AND ME

May 16, 1972, is a date that has no significant meaning to anyone but me and the Illinois Supreme Court because that was the date I was sworn in as a licensed attorney. The rest, as they say, is history. But along the way, many memorable experiences occurred as I represented the average guy or gal who happened to get into some legal mess. No corporate CEOs were in my clientele, no fund managers, just people you'd meet daily—teachers, cab drivers, laborers, and diverse occupations. They would become my clients in various ways. Some were referred to me by other attorneys who did not want to step foot in a courtroom. Some were generated through the firm where I worked; others were referrals from previous clients who thought I had done an excellent job. As varied as the sources were, the situations in which some of these people found themselves needed a lawyer to fight for them.

I started in a small firm, a three-person firm, principally involved in plaintiff's personal injury cases—car crashes, fall-down incidents, dog bites, work injuries, and other skirmishes requiring legal assistance.

My first day on the job couldn't have been more

uneventful, merely organizing my office. I had never walked into a law office or a courtroom before. I was fresh out of law school and had interviewed at a time when law jobs were scarce. Big firms didn't want newbies. I sensed the general attitude of the hiring partners in large firms was cold, if not dismissive. In a tight labor market, new attorneys hired would get the best training, work at the firm for a few years, and either move to another firm for more money or start their firms. Big firms wanted commitments since they were paying substantial beginning salaries.

The firm that hired me wanted me to handle cases that could not be settled through negotiation by the partners. If the case required filing a lawsuit, I would handle it, and I would receive a portion of the attorney's fees in addition to a nominal weekly salary.

When I showed up for work, I was busy placing books on the shelves in my office when the hiring partner came in and asked me what I was doing.

"I'm setting up my library," I said. "These are my reference books."

"Well," he said, "you'll never use any of them here."

That was my first taste of reality in the plaintiff's personal injury law business. I had no high expectations. That was my reality check and initiation into becoming a "trial attorney."

I was happy to get the job and figured I'd learn by doing, which was how most of my recently graduated friends started. Small firms try to churn settlements out of the cases we had. If a case could not be settled, I handled it. The firm didn't care about those cases, which, they figured, were lost causes anyway, if the case couldn't be settled without a lawsuit being filed. They gave me the throwaway instances, which were to become my caseload. Each was a challenge to weave straw into gold since I would receive some of the proceeds if I succeeded.

I had the task of gathering the documents and materials,

organizing them into a coherent presentation, preparing the complaint (which was the initial charge against the alleged at-fault party), creating the discovery materials, and taking statements from the parties, all in preparation for an arbitration hearing or a full-blown jury trial.

Discovery is the formal investigation of a filed lawsuit. Each side is entitled to send written questions to the opposing counsel, requests for documents to be produced, and requests for sworn statements and depositions of the parties. Those measures are governed by court rules to limit the issues in the case being prosecuted. The defendant seeks to determine the basis of the plaintiff's claim, and the plaintiff wants to flush out any defenses that will be presented.

Before that, I had yet to learn what went into that process. I had not taken a trial advocacy class in law school. Figuring I better know my tasks and how to do them, I enrolled in a private trial technique course with a noted trial attorney to learn the skills I would need to navigate the discipline of trying cases.

I had yet to complete the course when I walked into the office one morning, and my boss handed me a file jacket filled with random, unorganized documents I had never seen before. He said, "Here, get this case ready. You're on trial tomorrow morning." Then, just as abruptly, he left. Shocking would be a mild description of my emotions. Fear and terror were more appropriate. I worked on the file for hours and late into the night, arranging and reading all the documents, the pleadings, the discovery materials, and the sworn statements of the parties. In addition, I had to review all the medical records, reports, and bills to educate myself about my client's claimed injuries. Reading through the file, I discovered the case involved a rear end motor vehicle collision, from which my client claimed he was injured. Significant medical bills and photographs of his station wagon showed that the car's rear had been smashed and the window had broken out. I couldn't believe the partners had entrusted me with such a critical case.

The following day, my client appeared in my office, and we spent time going through the facts of the case, the injuries, and his current condition. He had a good memory of the events and spoke of his activities before and after the collision with clarity. He was dressed appropriately for an appearance in court. His demeanor, powers of recollection, and ability to recollect and describe the events was impressive. He would be an outstanding witness for himself. I felt a great sense of responsibility to him and my firm, and with the naive confidence of a young attorney who had never tried a case, we went to court.

We arrived in the courtroom, met the opposing attorney and the presiding judge, and discussed some preliminary issues. The judge was a seasoned jurist who could sense my nervousness and lack of comfort or familiarity with the process. He was very accommodating when I told him this was my first case.

After a while, we walked into the courtroom filled with thirty-six potential jurors. When a case is set for trial, the judge requests a pool of potential jurors from a holding room in the courthouse. A jury is usually made up of twelve jurors. Since each side can challenge a potential juror using preemptory challenges and some of the pool may have conflicts or be unable to serve for several reasons, the thirty-six is whittled down to the acceptable twelve and sometimes a couple of alternate jurors.

The selection process involved asking the potential jurors questions about their ability to be fair and impartial to both sides and to listen to the evidence presented in reaching their decision, which, by rule, required a unanimous verdict. Usually, the judge will ask some general questions. Then, each attorney can ask additional questions about qualifications, being mindful not to attempt to indoctrinate the jurors about the facts of the case.

After the first panel had been accepted, I was getting comfortable with the jury questioning and gained some confidence in my first jury trial experience. Looking back, I realize it was the lull before the storm.

My opponent was experienced in trying cases. He skillfully asked important questions about the jurors' qualifications and selected people to sit on the jury and decide the case. I didn't know what to ask or who to disqualify, but I agreed to accept those I felt would be fair and a good cross- section of society to hear my client's case.

I was confident about the liability in the case against the defendant. The collision involved a rear-end collision, where my client had stopped at a red light, and the defendant struck my client's vehicle. The defendant was negligent. The facts were clear, and I was getting comfortable with myself moving around the courtroom like I knew what I was doing. I gave a brief "opening" statement of what I thought the evidence would show and why my client should be well compensated for the injuries caused by the defendant's negligence, the at-fault driver. The defense attorney also gave a presentation, denying all my comments and asking the jurors to listen to all the evidence from both sides, not make any judgments until all the evidence had been presented, and reach a decision based on the evidence.

My client took the stand and was sworn in, and in response to my prepared questions, he described the sudden, violent crash and the impact that threw him around in his car. He spoke of the broken rear end of the vehicle and the shattered back window and, in stark detail, described the force of the impact. In addition, he stated that the impact caused the carburetor to malfunction, turning off the vehicle right at the point of impact, in the middle of the road. He talked about the injury he suffered. He claimed the collision was so severe that his head snapped backward, causing a bone to fracture and protrude from his neck, causing excruciating pain. He said he couldn't even move after the collision and needed assistance getting out of the vehicle.

As I listened to his testimony, I was nearly overcome with the enormity of my responsibility. I started thinking the firm entrusted this severe injury case to me, and getting my client a recovery weighed heavily on my conscience. I wanted to do the best job for this poor guy. The defense attorney asked almost the same set of questions of my client, confirming the collision, the impact, the injury, the bone protruding from his neck, and the disabled condition of the car.

I presented the medical evidence available to me, and I rested my case. Now, it was the defense attorney's turn to present his case.

"I call Chicago Police officer, star number…" he said, giving his name. A Chicago Police officer walked up to the witness stand in full regalia—uniform, badge, and a brisk and official demeanor. He was carrying some documents, which I expected to be the official police report. The officer stood, raised his right hand, and was sworn in by the clerk.

"Please state your name and position, Officer," the defense counsel asked. The officer responded. "Please tell the ladies and gentlemen of the jury your position and responsibilities." The officer gave a concise and detailed description of his training at the police academy, his beat, his work hours, and his years of training investigating and completing collision reports.

"Were you the officer who reported the incident, which is the subject matter of this lawsuit?" "Yes, I was."

"Do you have an independent recollection of the collision?" The law prevented him from reading the report, so this question allowed him to testify from his memory.

"Yes," he said, "I remember the entire incident."

"Would you please describe what you observed upon your

arrival at the scene?" "Yes, when I arrived, the gentleman at the plaintiff's table was standing by the side of his vehicle, which was stopped in the middle of the street. I asked him what had happened, and he said he was stopped in traffic when the other vehicle struck his car. The damaged cars were still touching." "Then what happened, Officer?" counsel inquired.

"The plaintiff told me that his car wouldn't start, so we went to the hood of his car, and the plaintiff showed me the distributor was cracked."

"Then what happened, Officer?"

"I told the plaintiff we would have to move the car out of traffic."

Then he said, "The plaintiff and I got on each side of the vehicle and pushed the plaintiff's vehicle about a half block down the street into a parking space."

I thought to myself, this can't be good. Then it got worse, if possible, and I could sense this case wasn't what I thought it was.

"At any time, did the plaintiff ever indicate he was in pain?"

"No."

"Did he tell you he was hurt, Officer?" "No."

"Did you sense he was suffering any pain at any time?" "No."

"Did you ever observe any injuries to his neck?" "No."

"Did the plaintiff ever show you a bone sticking out of his neck?"

"No."

"Did the plaintiff ever request an ambulance or any medical care?"

"No."

We made our closing arguments, and the judge instructed the jury on the law. I don't remember how long the jury was "deliberating," but I recall that the verdict came in before I walked the one block back to my office: not guilty.

When I reported the trial's outcome to the partner, he merely shrugged and told me not to worry about it; it wouldn't be my last loss. The firm was more satisfied that I had tried the case to a verdict.

Every jury trial is reported in the personal injury bar publications. Ironically, the fact that our firm tried a case to verdict would be noted by the insurance companies that track the data and establish our firm as a credible litigation firm.

To me, it was a sobering experience that taught me a lesson that not everything that, at first, seems to glitter is gold.

The Lottery

On an ordinary day, a couple called me for an appointment to discuss their problem with a collection agency. The overwhelming volume of my cases were the plaintiff's personal injury cases. The couple told me on the phone that a former client had given them my telephone number and that their friend had told them that if anyone could help them, it would be me. They came into my office the next day with a hospital bill for more than $80,000, which was the subject of a collection agency's harassing phone calls and notices of punitive action the collection agency would be taking against them. They didn't have any documentation about what the bill was for.

I listened to them explain that they didn't have health insurance or own any property and couldn't afford to pay the bill, even if they could enter a payment plan. I told them this was a case outside the types of cases I handled, and I didn't think I could help them with such a commercial collection matter.

During the interview, I could sense that the wife was answering all my questions, and her husband was sitting there with a blank, distant look. He was impaired in some way. I asked the man a few simple questions, which he couldn't answer. I sensed they were very desperate and felt obligated to try to assist them with the bill, thinking perhaps I could negotiate a reduction, so I asked the wife to give me more details about how they incurred such a large hospital bill.

She told me the couple owned and operated a franchise restaurant. During the previous summer, the air conditioner on the building's roof broke down. They called a contractor to come to their store and examine the air conditioning unit. The contractor went up on the roof, repaired the air conditioner, and called for the owner to come up, check that the air conditioner was fixed, and pay him.

The husband climbed up on the roof, on a ladder the contractor had erected against the wall of the store building. He checked that the air-conditioning unit was operating and gave the contractor a check. When it came time to come down off the roof, the ladder was three feet shorter than the roof line. When the husband started climbing the ladder, he missed the top rung and fell approximately twenty feet, suffering a severe head injury. He was taken to the hospital, treated, and released. The service charges were related to the fall and treatment for his head injury.

At the time of my conversation with the couple, a law for construction accidents required a contractor using a ladder, they had to set it up so the ladder extended at least three feet above the roof line. I informed the couple that they could sue the contractor for violating that law and try to recoup the cost of the hospital care. They agreed to retain my services to pursue that claim.

I prepared a lawsuit, filed it, and issued the suit papers to the sheriff to serve the contractor. The sheriff served the defendant/contractor, but he never filed an appearance or an answer. Despite my efforts to attract his attention and get him involved in the lawsuit, I heard nothing from the contractor for months to discover whether he had insurance.

The Lottery

When a person has been sued and served with the suit papers, they must appear within a specific time and file an answer or response to the charges. If they don't, a plaintiff may file a document requesting the court to enter a finding that the party is in default and the allegations in the complaint are confessed against them. After that, the suing party may appear before a judge, have the plaintiff testify on their behalf, and request a judgment be entered, which is precisely what I did.

Based on the testimony about the incident, the nature and extent of his brain injury, and the medical bills, including the hospital bill, which was still unpaid, we obtained a substantial default judgment. However, the decision was only as valuable as our ability to get the defendant contractor to come forward with an insurance policy or pay it out of his personal funds. So, all we had was a piece of paper.

Once a default order has been entered, after thirty days, the judgment becomes a final judgment. Then, the judgment creditor, my clients, could try to collect the judgment. Usually, a defaulted person who receives a copy of the default order or the judgment itself will hire a lawyer to appear and try to undo the judgment formally. The defendant can attack the initial service, deliver the lawsuit papers, or try to vacate the default judgment that had been entered. In my client's case, the defendant did nothing. Months passed, and we heard nothing from the defendant, even though I attempted to encourage him to contact me or retain counsel. I had no information on whether the defendant had insurance or assets, which I could attach.

About a year after we obtained the default judgment, my client's wife called my office. I recognized her voice, thinking she wanted a status report on the case. There was no progress, and I steeled myself to inform her of the bad news that if the defendant didn't have insurance, the judgment was only worth the paper it was written on. Instead, she told me there were rumors in her neighborhood about the contractor.

"What rumors?" I asked.

She said, "The people in the neighborhood think the contractor won the lotto, and he fled back to his home country."

I thought to myself, this can't possibly be true. Things like that don't ordinarily happen in the real world of personal injury law.

With great skepticism, I called an attorney I knew in the attorney general's office and asked, "How can I garnish the lotto?"

He told me he'd have to check the lottery's computer to see if the information was accurate and if the contractor won. If valid, I could issue a garnishment against the lottery office, and they would honor the judgment I had obtained.

About an hour later, after he checked the computer, he called. "Son of a bitch," he said. The guy had won a $2 million lottery prize, and the first installment payment was about to be paid. Lottery winnings can be paid in a discounted lump sum or yearly installments. This lottery winner had elected to take annual installments. I quickly prepared documents to file a garnishment action against the lottery, and within a very short time, I received papers from an international law firm contesting the judgment.

I never thought my skills as a lawyer would be tested so dramatically at such an early stage in my career, facing the artillery that an internationally renowned firm might bring. The next step in the process of what happened next needs some explanation. When this all transpired, an attorney who wished to attack a judgment could do so in one of two ways. One way is to file a paper attacking the validity of service of the suit papers. That's referred to as a motion to quash service. That strategy goes to the issue of due process. If the service is shown to be defective, the default judgment falls, and you must start from scratch. The defendant is not submitting themselves to the court's jurisdiction.

The other method of attack is to request the judgment be vacated. That attack doesn't question the issue of due process but accepts that service was adequate and the judgment is valid, but there are defenses to the judgment.

The difference between the two approaches is that the second one submits the defendant to the court's jurisdiction, whereas the former doesn't.

The error here is that the international firm with a big reputation requested the judgment be vacated, so our judgment against the defendant was based on good service. I'll never forget the sage words of the judge listening to their arguments, "Welcome, Counsel, to the Circuit Court of Cook County, Illinois."

I informed my clients of these developments, and they were thrilled that the judgment would be enforced.

After some discussions and intense negotiations, we entered a settlement of the judgment, whereby the government took a percentage off the top of the award (the contractor/defendant was a foreign national, and the government took a cut off the top of any lottery payment for taxes). The remaining amounts were divided in half between my client, me, and the contractor. For the next twenty years, on August 22 of every year, my clients and I received a check from the Illinois Lottery without fail. We resolved the hospital bill on a payment plan, and my clients were able to pay for a new house, their son's college education, and some semblance of peace of mind for their disabled husband and father. Although I never spoke about the case, friends and colleagues around the courthouse got wind of my lottery case, which became part of the folklore in my practice. I could not have been more proud as a lawyer.

Truth Is Stranger than Fiction:

Colorful judges were sitting in our courthouse; one was a little wackier than the others. His reputation as an oddball preceded his being elevated to the bench. As the story went, I heard third- or fourth-hand that before he became an attorney, he was a sailor in the Navy and had been stationed in the Pacific during WWII. He would conduct card games on slow days at sea and owned a green velvet tablecloth on which he and the other sailors would play cards.

At the end of the war, when the signing of the surrender of the Japanese was to take place on board his ship, his commanding officer wanted to enhance the ceremonies by covering the table on which the signing was to take place with a tablecloth, to dress it up for the occasion. The commander knew of the tablecloth being on board. So, he went to the sailor and asked to use the tablecloth. The sailor refused. "I won't do it. I'll never see it again." The officer pleaded with the sailor to no avail. Regardless of the argument, he would not give up his tablecloth.

So, as wacky as the situation was, the commanding officer

sent the ship's captain to plead to use the tablecloth. No way, he was not giving it up.

Finally, the admiral of the fleet, who was to participate in the signing ceremony, came down below to see the sailor with the tablecloth. According to the reports, admittedly hearsay, the admiral told the sailor that if he didn't let them use the tablecloth for this historic event, he would order him to clean every lavatory on every ship in the fleet with a toothbrush.

Reluctantly, faced with that threat, the tablecloth was handed over.

So, when the sailor became an attorney and then was elevated to the bench, his tendency to do some wacky things was almost a certainty.

At one term, he had an announced goal of presiding over the most jury trials in one year of any judge in the history of the courthouse. The magic number he sought was sixty trials in one year—a near impossibility.

During his quest, from time to time, he would announce, at the opening of the daily court call, "Anyone who settles a case today gets a cigar." It was improper, but he gave away a lot of cigars. On another occasion, a jury trial was underway, over which he was presiding. The case had concluded and had been submitted to the jury for deliberations. The jury was sequestered for their deliberations in a jury room adjacent to the courtroom. Usually, a judge awaits the entry of its verdict before a new trial begins. Not in his courtroom. He was on a quest. So, he called for another case while the first jury was still deliberating and before they had reached a verdict. The rules are very well established: once a jury has been sworn in and hears the evidence in a case, the judge reads the jurors the law to be applied to the facts presented by the witnesses. The jurors are submitted to the care and supervision of a sheriff, who sequesters them in a room for their deliberations. They are not to be disturbed or interfered with in any way until they reach their verdict. Juries are then locked into a room and deliberate until they have reached their verdict. The jurors' deliberations can get heated occasionally, and voices can get loud.

While the second jury was being questioned for the subsequent trial, the deliberations in the jury room from the previous case became very loud, and it was clear there were arguments among the jurors. The judge, counsel, and prospective new jurors could hear the arguing in the courtroom.

Without missing a beat and in a fit of apparent rage, the judge rose from his seat, marched over to the door of the jury room, pushed aside the bailiff, knocked loudly, opened the jury room door, and to everyone's amazement, yelled, "Shut up! There's another trial going on out here." Everyone, including the sheriff, was stunned at the outburst, and then he returned to his seat and calmly said, "Carry on." Unheard of.

Legend has it that during a trial, this same jurist would habitually turn his chair around to face the wall behind him, and he tended to fall asleep. The attorneys trying the case were questioning a witness on the stand, and they and the jurors realized the judge was asleep. One of the questions from the plaintiff's counsel prompted an objection from the defense lawyer. "I object," said the defense attorney. Nothing. No response from the judge. A few moments went by, and still no response from the judge. "I object," the defense attorney repeated. No ruling was forthcoming. Both attorneys and the jurors realized the situation.

The plaintiff's attorney said, "Go, wake him up."

The defense counsel said, "I won't wake him up. You wake him up." The plaintiff's counsel said, "It's your objection. You wake him up." At this point, some jurors gathered the humor in the situation and started to laugh, which awakened the judge, who was startled. He said, "What was the last question?" At this point, the court reporter read the last question and the objection, the court made a ruling, and the trial concluded.

My last and most memorable event with this judge came during a hearing on a default jury prove-up. By way of explanation, I represented a lady in a car crash with another driver. After the suit was filed, the sheriff served the defendant with the suit papers. The defendant filed an appearance for herself (pro se) and demanded a six-person jury. Then, the defendant did nothing. She did not file an answer or respond to any of the proceedings. I prepared and filed a request for an order of default against her. After the default order was entered, the case was set for proof of the allegations in the lawsuit. At the time, the local rules provided that the prove-up had to be conducted before a six-person jury, even if no defendant was present.

The case was assigned to this wacky judge. On the day of the prove-up, I advised my client about the quirks of the judge and that she could request a change of judge to decide the case, but she wanted to conclude the case, so we decided to proceed.

When we arrived at the courtroom, the clerk retrieved the file and gave it to the judge sitting in his chambers. After briefly reviewing the file documents, he called me back into his chambers. He asked me a few questions about the case and told me to wait in the courtroom while he called for a panel of jurors to be brought to the courtroom.

Usually, a judge would request enough potential jurors for the handling attorney to question the panel and either accept or discharge them. There are different challenges an attorney could make if they feel the juror is not able to be fair and impartial. If the trial attorney doesn't regard them as suitable for the type of case being presented, a peremptory challenge can exclude them. So, with considerable disbelief, six juror candidates entered the courtroom for questioning. They were seated, and the judge asked me, "Do you want to ask them questions?"

"What's the point?" I answered. If I had disqualified any of the six potential jurors, getting more jurors for questioning would have taken hours. So, I accepted the six.

"Do you want to make an opening statement?" the judge asked.

I stood before the jurors and began, "Ladies and gentlemen of the jury, you've been called to sit and listen to this case as a default. My client sued the defendant for negligence. The defendant's vehicle struck my client's vehicle when stopped at a red traffic light, and the plaintiff was injured. I believe the evidence we intend to present through the testimony of my client and the documents we shall offer into evidence will persuade you to enter a judgment against the defendant. We filed this lawsuit, and the defendant was served with the lawsuit papers. The defendant filed a jury demand, but she didn't participate in the case, so a default order was entered against her, which was done by rule. So, your task will be to listen to the evidence and render a verdict.

"This proceeding isn't intended to punish the defendant but to seek justice for her negligence and fair and reasonable compensation for her injuries. My client claims she was injured as a result of the negligence of the defendant."

I provided the details of the crash and the injuries she was claiming and argued that my client was entitled to receive fair and reasonable payment for her losses. The plaintiff took the stand, was sworn in, and testified about the crash, the injuries, her care and treatment, and the damage to her car. She had incurred about $2,500 in medical care, and we submitted those bills into evidence in the case. She also had photographs of her car, which were entered into evidence as proof of the severity of the impact. We also submitted the property damage of $1,200, and we rested our case.

The judge asked me, "Do you wish to give a closing argument?" I did and stood to give a short closing argument.

"Ladies and gentlemen, as I informed you at the start of this trial, this proceeding isn't to punish the defendant but to provide fair and reasonable compensation to my client for the damages that the defendant's negligence caused," I started.

"The evidence has shown that the defendant was not paying attention to her driving, not keeping a proper lookout for other cars, and crashed into the plaintiff's vehicle. The collision caused the property damages and injuries we told you about in our opening statement. You heard the sworn testimony from the plaintiff in support of her claim. Now that the evidence has been presented, it is your sworn duty to weigh the evidence presented and reach a fair verdict in her favor."

I proceeded, "I am not here to tell you what the award should be. It should be fair and reasonable and compensate the plaintiff for all her damages. From my experience trying cases like this, I could only provide you with my suggestion as to what that award should be. Still, you may decide any amount justified by the evidence you heard when you deliberate."

I continued, "To me, a fair and reasonable amount to compensate her for her injuries and damages would be $10,000."

Without missing a beat, the judge blurted out, "Aw, come on, Leo, don't you think that's a little high? Don't you think you should bring that down?"

My life and career began to flash before my eyes. Standing in front of the jury, I was astonished, and all I could say was, "I don't think I have to know, Judge."

Sheepishly, I thanked the jury and sat down.

The jury concluded with a verdict on the medical bills and property damage only, and the rest was history.

Leo Bleiman

I am the only attorney who lost a default jury prove-up in the history of that courthouse.

Lifesaver

In the personal injury business, one of the crucial rules which the parties must comply is the statute of limitations. It's a simple rule. Within a set time after an injury occurs, a person must file a lawsuit by the time the statute of limitations expires or they would lose their case as untimely. Without going into the details of the purpose behind the rule, it is legal malpractice not to adhere to that time rule. Usually, for auto collisions and falls, the time limit is two years. There are exceptions for cases against municipalities, government operations, and others for medical negligence cases.

There are also practical considerations that go into the decision to file a lawsuit or not. Some of the attorneys who referred cases to me would delay filing and try to negotiate a settlement almost to the day the statute expired. It costs money to file a lawsuit, which most clients don't have. If the case must be filed, many attorneys try to avoid going to court, so they need to get the consent of their client to refer the matter to an experienced attorney who tries cases, and with the referral of the case, the original attorney and the trial attorney share a percentage of any award. So, economics plays a part in whether and when to refer the case to another attorney.

I had such an arrangement with an attorney who would always wait until a month or so before the expiration of the statute of limitations to contact me about cases he could not settle and didn't want to file himself. A client of his had fallen from a roof and suffered a severe leg fracture. The injury resulted in major surgery and enormous bills for care and treatment, which were unpaid.

The facts of the case were simple enough. The building owner had hired the client to tuck-point the side of a building. The owner was the general contractor who obtained a permit for the work and supervised its performance.

The tuck-pointed wall was situated next to a lower building, and the workman was using the roof of the adjacent building to set up a ladder to do the work. The tuck-pointed wall extended up about 20 feet and ran the entire length of the lot, about 125 feet. The size of the roof of the adjacent building was around 100 feet.

As circumstances occurred, the tuck-pointer would work on the ladder and tuck-point the top of the wall along the length of the shorter building until he got to the end and then get down from the ladder and continue to tuck-point the wall standing on the roof next door. He was tuck-pointing and paying attention to the work, and he continued to do so, paying attention to his work. As he moved along the wall he was working on, he was so intent on the work that he walked off the end of the lower building, fell 20 feet to the ground, and fractured his leg in several places.

The statute of limitations for any potential case was expiring. The attorney handling the case either didn't know if there was a viable cause of action or who to sue, and he called me to ask if I would be interested in investigating a possible injury claim. He admitted that he was about to drop the case since he couldn't think of a lawsuit, he could bring for anyone's negligence. He thought the tuck-pointer was the sole cause of the incident.

Since there was such mounting pressure, the lawyer gave me the client's name, and I called him to ask some questions about how the incident occurred. He was somewhat surprised that a lawsuit had not been filed already because in the months that had gone by, he'd had surgeries and therapy and mounting unpaid medical bills, and he had yet to return to work.

I obtained the address of the building, and I went there to view the scene. It was apparent what had happened, and there was clear evidence that there was a cause of action to pursue against the owner of the building. Usually, at a construction site, the areas of potential fall risks are taped or barricaded so workers are made aware of the end of a work area. Some photographs showed that this construction site didn't have those in place. The owner, acting as the general contractor, could be held liable under a law that was in effect at the time for structural work.

I immediately filed a lawsuit, presented the facts of the occurrence to the insurance carrier and their appointed attorneys, and showed them the photographs I had obtained of the scene. My client gave his deposition, and within a few months, I negotiated a significant settlement of the lawsuit, pay all the outstanding medical bills, and compensate the worker.

From and after the conclusion of that case, the referring attorney regularly consulted with me on matters with legal issues he needed more time and expertise to handle, and our professional relationship continued to grow.

Anecdotally, occasionally, I would drive past those buildings on the way home from work, and I proudly recall the work I did on that case.

Time Matters

In the simplest explanation, the applicable statute of limitations in medical negligence cases is two years from the alleged medically negligent act or two years from the date the patient discovers the care or treatment they received was careless, but within four years of the negligent treatment. Before filing a medical negligence claim, the threshold requirement is having a report prepared by a physician practicing in the same field of medicine who has reviewed the relevant medical records. The report must determine and provide the opinion that, based upon a reasonable degree of medical and scientific certainty, a reasonable and meritorious cause of action exists and that the allegedly negligent physician failed to conform to the standards of acceptable medical practice, which failure caused the claimed injury.

In addition to the physician's report, the attorney seeking to file a complaint must sign an affidavit attesting to the consultation with a qualified physician who has provided the opinion that negligence occurred. Once those documents are available, an attorney may file a claim for medical negligence.

I was introduced to a suburban attorney by a mutual friend. The attorney had an active, well-respected commercial and business practice, which was the primary function of the practice. His firm had a young associate who handled the firm's personal injury cases. A few months before I became involved, the firm's partner was concerned that the associate's erratic behavior jeopardized the firm's cases. He thought his associate was having a nervous breakdown, and he was worried that the cases in the office weren't being kept current. Most of the cases were common automobile collisions. The firm wanted me to do an inventory of the cases and provide them with a summary of the status of each case.

On a cold, wintry Saturday morning, I drove the sixty miles to their office and examined each file. Although most files were routine automobile cases, there were a few work injury files and several larger files. After a few hours of reviewing the more minor cases, I determined the status of each was in relatively satisfactory condition. I could easily organize and dispose of them if the clients signed written consent for my participation. I was assured the firm's clients had the utmost trust and confidence in the firm, and they would allow me to enter an appearance and handle the cases to their conclusion.

One of the larger files gave me cause for concern, and I called the partner who had asked me for my review and opinion. A complaint had been filed for a widow whose husband had died. The complaint was almost perfunctory. It was three or four pages long, with sparse details and generalized allegations of negligence by a doctor. The complaint did not have a physician's report attached nor an affidavit from the attorney. An affidavit was attached, which was allowed by the rules, stating that the attorney could not obtain a physician's report within the appropriate time for filing and requested additional time to get such a report. That was permitted at the time. However, there was another issue of concern. The complaint was filed the day before the applicable statute of limitations expired at 4:30 p.m. The affidavit was time-stamped by the clerk's office at 8:30 a.m. the next day, which would be untimely.

After reading the complaint, I immediately grew concerned. In the file, in the same folder as the filed complaint, was an eight-page, single-spaced, typed, moment-by-moment history of what had happened to the deceased husband, written by the widow. The narrative was spellbinding, and I read it twice to ensure I understood all the details.

The widow wrote that her husband was a forty-year-old overweight, beer-bellied smoker. He had left work not feeling very well. It was winter. The husband had worked the entire day in the cold and continued not feeling well; he was sweating profusely in a T-shirt, with chest pains and pain down his left arm. His wife told him to go to an emergency room, but he insisted he'd stop at an outpatient facility before he came home.

He stopped at a local outpatient treatment center, where he waited, still sweating, in a T-shirt, in frigid weather, still having chest pains and pains shooting down his arm. He gave the doctor on call a complete history, which was recorded in his intake chart. An EKG was performed, which was interpreted as "not normal," and the doctor who examined him told him, "I can't rule out you may be having a heart attack, but I'm going to give you some 'heart pills.' Take these and go to the hospital on Monday [this was Friday] for a stress test." He took the pills from the physician, left the clinic, and drove home, still sweating, in a T-shirt, with chest and arm pain.

When he arrived home, his wife asked him numerous questions, which he answered, and then she had him lie in bed to rest. Within three hours of his arrival, he died. The coroner determined that he died of a massive heart attack.

After reading the tragic details, I realized this case was in dire jeopardy of being dismissed, exposing the firm to colossal liability. I told the partner the sad news:

The filing issues.

The problems in the complaint.

There is a lack of a timely stamped request for an extension to file the physician's report.

I laid it all out.

The following day, the partner, the widow, and I met at the office and explained the situation to her. She was surprisingly calm when she heard the news and was sympathetic toward the associate who had caused the problems. She had met him on occasion and had prepared the summary I read at the associate's request. She expressed hope that the associate would get professional help. She also agreed to allow me to become involved in the case against the doctor by signing a consent for my participation.

My first task was to correct the record about the late-filed affidavit and then get a physician's report. I prepared a document to substitute for the former attorney of record and set up a hearing, which, as expected, prompted the defense attorney to file a motion to dismiss the complaint in its entirety. On the day of the hearing on both motions, I had a tremendous feeling of doom stepping up before a judge who I'd never appeared before. I was in a courthouse I'd rarely been in, arguing before a judge I had never seen or argued any cases. I was in a jurisdiction more sympathetic to local attorneys than interlopers like me.

When our case was called, I had priority in presenting my motion to appear and substitute for the previous attorney, and then the opposing counsel argued his motion on timeliness. In my response, I directed the judge to the file stamp markings on the complaint and the attorney's affidavit. The complaint and affidavit were stapled together, but only the complaint had a time stamp. I explained my theory of what had happened when the complaint and affidavit were filed and time-stamped.

I said, "If you look at the time stamp and the fact that they were stapled together, the filing time was minutes before the clerk's office closed." I continued, "What probably happened was that the clerk overlooked the affidavit attached to the complaint, and she only stamped the top of the first page.

When she came in the following day, at 8:30 a.m., she may have noticed the affidavit was not time-stamped, so she stamped it then."

Without batting an eye, after I stopped talking, the judge leaned over to the court clerk sitting next to him and asked, "Could that have happened?"

To which she replied, "Sure, it happens a lot. Just inadvertence."

With that, the judge denied the defense motion, and I was allowed time to amend the complaint, adding more facts, a physician's report, my affidavit, and the case was allowed to proceed. Statistics show that 80 percent or more of medical negligence cases have no award from juries. There are many factors. Defense attorneys have fraternities of physicians available to them to dispute whatever theory of negligence a plaintiff may bring. The plaintiff's attorney often struggles to find a credible, knowledgeable physician whose opinion is rock solid and incontrovertible. My work was cut out for me.

Eventually, someone put me in contact with a practicing internal medicine physician who offered to review the records. However, at the outset, he informed me that he would only write a report if the records were rock-solid regarding the physician's negligence and failure to abide by the standard of care.

A month later, I received his report, in which he categorically stated that upon reading the EKG, which was deemed "abnormal" by the physician who had examined my client's husband, it was apparent that the husband was having a cardiac event while he was in the examination!

I prepared an amended complaint and attached his report

and my affidavit. In the discovery deposition of the physician charged with negligence, she admitted that she could not rule out a cardiac event, a multiple vessel occlusion in the husband's heart, which was the cause of his death. The defendant's attorney deposed my client, the widow, and she testified about every detail in the personal depiction she had prepared, which was as emotional as you might imagine. He had died in her arms. They had two children who were devastated by their father's loss.

After a few months of discussions, the widow, my referring attorney, and I resolved the case for a substantial amount.

That's usually the end of the relationship in the personal injury litigation world, but this case was far from over. After receiving the settlement funds, the widow quit her job, enrolled in college, and became a librarian. Her children were seventeen and nineteen. The nineteen-year-old daughter took some of her funds, bought some necessities, and deposited most of them into government-secured funds, setting her up for life.

We allotted some money for the seventeen-year-old's use and placed the other funds in a trust for his protection. In cases where a minor is injured or receives money from any recovery, the rules require attorneys to place the funds into an account in the minor's name, which are to remain subject to any withdrawal requests only to be done by order of the court. Children can access their money by applying to the court for a withdrawal up to the age of their majority, at age eighteen. Usually, the court can only counsel an eighteen-year-old not to squander the money but can't prevent them from access to it. From our experience, this protects the minor's interests from their parents wasting the money and from a minor's carelessness in depleting the funds.

We sensed the minor son was irresponsible and placed the funds into a locked account with the mother's consent, which would only be available for him to withdraw at age twenty-five.

Our suspicions were correct. Within thirty days of receiving the proceeds we had allotted for his "personal use," he had spent all the funds given to him and wanted to break the trust, which was under his mother's control, or he would have squandered it all.

There is another side to this story that bears mentioning. Usually, once a case concludes, we rarely hear from the parties and rarely from any of the witnesses. In this case, a few years after the case was over, I received a telephone call from our expert witness, who had furnished the physician's report. His report was the key to our success. His call was completely unexpected.

He reminded me of his participation in the case, for which I thanked him again, and I asked why he was calling. He told me that he had just seen a patient in his emergency room and had read an EKG of his patient. The gentleman had arrived at the emergency department with symptoms related to chest pains, and my expert examined him and ordered an EKG, the electronic tracing of the patient's heart rhythm.

When the doctor read the EKG, he noticed the exact tracing he had remembered seeing on the case I had asked him to review. Upon recognizing that tracing, he determined the new patient had a cardiac episode. The doctor administered clot-busting drugs, which had an immediate effect, and the patient left the emergency room. The patient's attack was confirmed once the blood enzyme analysis was available. Eventually, the patient was successfully treated as an outpatient and completely recovered.

The doctor told me the glitch was subtle, and had it not been for his participation in my case, noticing that glitch in the EKG (which is not ordinarily diagnostic), he might have missed the correct diagnosis, and the patient could have left the emergency room only to suffer the same fate as my former client's husband.

WORK-RELATED BASEBALL GAME:

One area of my practice involved representing workers injured on the job. When a person is injured during their employment, and the incident that injured them arises out of and during their employment, they are entitled to apply for an adjustment of claim at the Illinois Workers' Compensation Commission. The state set up the system to compensate victims of work injuries, and it was organized as a no-fault system, so long as the person's incident and injuries were causally related to the work they did.

Removing fault as an issue was traded off for limited benefits to the workers. An injured person is to be paid while off work under a doctor's care, and they would be paid based on a percentage of what they earned in their usual and customary job. There were several areas of benefits. According to a coding system, healthcare benefits are set by a medical fee schedule, establishing reimbursement levels for providers caring for injured workers' treatment.

The legislature established the payment of temporary total disability (TTD) benefits to preserve income for injured workers who cannot work due to a work-related injury. Those

WORK-RELATED BASEBALL GAME:

benefits are paid at a rate of two-thirds of a person's average weekly wage, defined generally as the average wage for a forty-hour work week, calculated based on a worker's earnings for the year before the date of the work injury. After the worker has reached a level of recovery that allows them to return to work, payment of permanent partial disability (PPD) benefits is paid and is calculated at 60 percent of a worker's average weekly wage.

The legislature assigned arbitrary values to various parts of the body for specific losses. Hands, arms, feet, legs, hearing loss, and vision impairment all have attributed values. There was another category of nonspecific areas, like back and neck injuries. The legislature also established a table of maximum benefit amounts indicating a specific number of weeks of disability assigned to each body part.

It was relatively easy to determine if a worker had suffered a work-related injury, which could result in a claim. If they fractured their arm doing their work at a place where they were assigned and it happened during work hours, their supervisor witnessed it, or if the worker reported the incident promptly, it would ordinarily be covered. There are exceptions to every rule, and each circumstance must be evaluated on its merit.

One case I handled for a woman raised numerous compensability issues. The woman was an unmarried, college-educated accountant/bookkeeper hired as a contract employee by a company to do a specific task for a set amount of money. Her contract was set to expire on August 1. She recorded her work hours but was off the company's regular payroll that had contracted with her.

The company had organized and participated in an intermural, coed softball league during the summer. The team needed an even mix of men and women in every game. The team needed another woman to participate in the league championship game, or they would be forced to forfeit. My client was not participating in the league, had never been on the team, had no uniform, and had never played in a single game throughout the summer. She never even attended one of the games. She was a bookworm and not the least bit athletic.

The championship game was set to start at 7:00 p.m. My client was still working on her assignment at the office when she received a call from a coworker. The team needed another woman to play in the championship game, or they would forfeit. She was told she needed to get to the park to fulfill the gender balance of the team. Reluctantly, she agreed to go, drove more than ten miles to get to the park, and arrived in time before the game started. She was assigned to right field, given a glove, and told to stand out during the game.

As the game proceeded, my client was the last batter on the roster. She never practiced, swung a bat, or touched a ball. During the game, she didn't catch any ball that was hit. The game reached the middle innings. It was her turn to bat. She swung and missed a couple of pitches. When the third pitch came at her, with her eyes closed, she swung and hit a ball into the outfield. She initially screamed and started running, with the coaches cheering her on, and she reached first base. The outfielder was still chasing after the ball in the outfield, which prompted the first base coach to urge my client to continue running to second base. So, my client tagged first base and took off toward second. As she approached second base, she slid onto her side, and her foot came into contact with a metal post sticking up from the ground. The impact caused injuries to her knee. She was bleeding and in severe pain. She couldn't stand or place any weight on her injured leg. She needed immediate medical care.

Someone from the team called an ambulance, which arrived at the park, drove onto the field, placed her on a gurney, and took her to a local hospital. She was admitted through the emergency department, and after diagnostic testing, it was determined that she had torn ligaments in her leg. She met with an orthopedic specialist, who recommended immediate surgery. After surgery, a few days in the hospital, and training on crutches, she was discharged, having incurred thousands of dollars in medical expenses.

She was off work and involved in physical therapy for months. The company refused to pay any of the bills and denied my client's right to workers' compensation benefits. They asserted that my client was not an employee and was not in the course and scope of her employment, claimed she was injured while engaged in a recreational activity after work hours, and that the Workers' Compensation Act did not cover the accident.

My client called me, still on crutches and wearing a cast on her leg that extended from her thigh to her foot. She brought me dozens of bills and collection notices from the healthcare providers. The company refused to pay expenses and gave her no reason when approaching them. She had questions about any claims she could bring to cover the costs. She was out of work, her rent and utilities were due, and she had no money after depleting her savings. She was desperate for help.

As I listened to her story, I realized there were numerous daunting legal questions about any claim. She asked if she could bring a lawsuit against the park. Could she sue the league? Did she have a claim under the Workers' Compensation Act? How was she going to get through this? I went through the facts of her case in detail several times. I needed to delve into precise details of her job, including how she was hired, paid, and by whom. I needed to know if there was a written contract about her assignment. I also asked about how she became involved in the baseball game and the circumstances of her injury.

I anticipated problems with any case we might file. I explained that a lawsuit against the park district would be problematic. Lawsuits against municipal corporations were lengthy, costly, and complex to prove. The Park district could argue they weren't willfully culpable, had no notice of any defect in sufficient time to repair it, and that a claim of mere negligence wouldn't carry the day. Municipalities have immunities that they could interpose against a negligence claim. We would have to prove that the park district operated their premises willfully and recklessly, consciously disregarding her safety. I didn't believe a case could be brought up, so I advised her accordingly.

We then discussed the concept of a workers' compensation claim. I explained that the probable reason the company was not paying for her medical expenses was their argument that she was engaged in what was commonly referred to as a "voluntary recreational activity," which, under the act and case law, would not arise out of or in the course of employment. The exception to that rule would be in cases where the employer or participation ordered participation to be mandatory.

Even if we could prove she had all the trappings of an "employee" and not an independent contractor, we would have the burden of proving her participation in the baseball game was mandatory.

We applied adjustment of the claim, the initial pleading in a workers' compensation claim. Those claims are filed with the Illinois Workers' Compensation Commission and are handled as administrative hearings before arbitrators, who hear the evidence and render awards for or against a worker. If either party is dissatisfied with the arbitrator's decision, they may file for a review by the commissioners, who act as appeals type of process. After that review, there are other and further consequences and procedures, which are beyond the necessity of explaining here. There are no discovery tools available in workers' compensation cases. Most of the time, the parties exchange relevant documents, like medical records and reports. If either side wishes to confirm or deny the nature or extent of the injuries, they may retain an examining physician, whose report may be admitted into evidence at arbitration.

I gathered the information I received from my client and scheduled the arbitration case as soon as possible. The company retained counsel who raised the defenses I anticipated. They claimed that my client wasn't an employee and that she was engaged in a voluntary recreational activity and raised the issue of the nature and extent of the injuries, claiming they weren't as disabling as my client claimed. They also claimed that the treatment she received, including the surgery, wasn't reasonable or necessary and that the expenses were not fair or reasonable. At trial, my client testified to her job duties and responsibilities, hours, work location, and wages. She worked out of the company offices, the company set her hours, the company paid for her wages under her contract, and she had an identification security badge to enter the premises where she worked. Occasionally, she was directed to visit the company's clients off-premises and would be reimbursed for her travel expenses. The company retained the right to terminate the contract.

In my estimation, we argued that all the attributes of her employment applied to her relationship with the company. They wanted to label her an independent contractor to avoid liability for her work-related injuries.

As for the defense argument that this was a voluntary recreational activity, we had to show that her participation in the baseball game was a condition of her employment. Recreational activities that the employer mandates could be compensable.

My client testified about the day she was called to participate in the baseball game. She was at work and preparing to leave for the day. She received a call from her supervisor, who pleaded with her to attend the game. The supervisor told her of their predicament, with a potential forfeiture of the title if they didn't have enough women players. My client asked what she would do; she didn't play baseball and had no equipment, shoes, gloves, or uniform. My client wasn't on the rosters for any of the previous games. When I received a copy of the tournament rule book, it confirmed that all the teams needed equal male and female players for each game.

When my client arrived at the game, her name was written on the scorecard by hand for the championship game. The team manager (my client's supervisor) kept the box score. The manager didn't even know my client's correct name and never asked her directly. She was on the score sheet under a name spelled differently altogether. I wondered if any other score sheets had my client's name on them, and the team manager admitted she wasn't. I asked if my client had a team uniform, and again, I received a negative response. Then I asked if my client had her glove, and he agreed that she was loaned a fielder's glove for the game and a team shirt to wear.

At the arbitration hearing, the team manager testified as a witness for the company, and he produced a neatly typed spreadsheet with the details of the game. He went through the details of the game, inning by inning, and his attorney offered the spreadsheet as evidence to prove my client did not participate in the game. He testified that all the listed team members volunteered to play and that my client's story about the game and her recruitment was fabricated.

I harkened back to my youthful baseball playing when I began my cross-examination. A designated scorer kept every score sheet and would make entries as the game progressed. Every player is listed on the roster, and every inning's progress is entered in real-time as it occurred. They are written on a sheet with the names and positions of each player, and their performance is charted by inning, hits, outs, and runs. I had

WORK-RELATED BASEBALL GAME:

never seen a scorecard kept at a baseball game on an Excel spreadsheet. I questioned the preparation of the handwritten scorecard and who possessed and controlled that document. He admitted ownership and possession of the original.

I asked the manager if he had prepared the documents he had presented. He admitted they were his entries. I wondered how he made the entries. He told the arbitrator and counsel that he took his handwritten score sheets to their office, took the data from the handwritten version, transferred it to an Excel program, and then printed it out for submission at the trial. My client's correctly spelled name did not appear on the spreadsheet.

Furthermore, there was a name like hers, but that could not be explained. We argued that the misspelled name indicated that my client had been recruited at the last minute and that no one knew her correct name. Still, she served their purpose by being a woman they needed to fulfill the number of women required to participate in the contest.

When any witness is sworn on oath and testifies about specific facts, the arbitrator's task is to evaluate their testimony, truthfulness, and credibility. Once their credibility has been damaged or destroyed during cross-examination, any testimony by that witness receives serious scrutiny.

I asked the witness to produce the original documents of the other games he'd scored. He didn't have them with him. He also needed the original, handwritten scorecard from the championship game.

When he couldn't produce the original scorecard, I objected to the Excel spreadsheet version, which the arbitrator then barred from being admitted into evidence.

The rule applicable to that objection is based on a legal principle known as the "best evidence" rule. Suppose the original of a document exists and is not produced by the person who has custody and control of the document. In that case, the judge or arbitrator can strike the substituted document. The company had sole custody and possession of the original, handwritten scorecards, so the arbitrator denied the company from using the spreadsheet version. We won. My client received an award of all her back pay, a percentage of her leg on an industrial basis for the nature and extent of her injuries, and payment of her healthcare expenses.

Call Alarm

The miracle of modern medicine has enriched our lives in ways unimaginable only a few years ago. Each discovery has enabled us to live longer, be more productive, and have enjoyable lives. With those advances, the reality of extended life expectancies has created issues not previously anticipated. People are living beyond their ability to care for themselves, creating an industry euphemistically called "senior living."

Facilities have been built to house the senior population nationwide, creating a huge financial windfall for developers and managers. These are not the "nursing homes" of the past. Many are high-end, well-maintained facilities with amenities you'd find at pricey resorts. Professional staff provide therapy sessions and guided field trips, engage the residents in recreational activities, prepare and serve meals, and make efforts for a meaningful senior lifestyle.

Many of these facilities provide care depending on the resident's abilities and are divided into independent living, assisted living, and custodial care. Another widely developing group is "memory care" facilities.

One feature of most of those facilities is a multi-tiered

safety system. At the entry doorways of the apartments are tags or indicators. At night, personnel would place the indicator into the "up" position. When the door is opened in the morning, the indicator will lower, signifying the resident is out of their apartment or room.

Another device in every hospital and senior living facility is a call button attached to a cord that, when pulled, alarms the management office that a resident is in distress.

My elderly client lived alone in an independent apartment in one of those facilities. She was in relatively good health but had a history of occasional reported falls. One night, she awoke to visit the bathroom, and as she sat down, she missed the commode and fell between the toilet and the adjacent bathtub. She could not extricate herself from her predicament and was lodged in the facilities. She repeatedly pulled on the bathroom alarm cord, with no response. Hours passed until about eleven in the morning, when the security staff noticed she hadn't left her apartment. The staff called the management office, and an attendant retrieved a key to the apartment and found my client. An ambulance was called, and she was taken to the hospital for treatment of severe bruises and a hip injury.

Her family contacted me to investigate and make a claim for her injuries against the building management and the alarm system company.

The incident details were simple, but the fault for the alarm failure was convoluted. The management and alarm company became embattled in a finger-pointing defense. I proceeded against both without caring who was responsible. Was it poor supervision? Why didn't security notice she hadn't left her apartment early in the morning during rounds? Why didn't the alarm sound in the management office?

The alarm company defended that its equipment was fully operational and produced records that indicated the entire system was checked twice a year, with the last check occurring just a few months before.

My argument was simple. In a situation where the safety and security of the residents depended upon a working alarm system, it needed to be checked daily, not semiannually. What kind of "safety" would be provided when the alarm system for these elderly residents required ready access to report any problems? More communication is needed if checked only every six months. I achieved a settlement, and the alarm system was converted to a daily check for the entire alarm system.

No Grit

Through a confluence of unusual circumstances, a large corporation hired me to defend them in a lawsuit alleging they were negligent in placing a floor surface in a car dealership. The plaintiff claimed he suffered debilitating back injuries and multiple surgeries, which provided him with no relief, and he was in constant, unbearable pain. He claimed he could never work again due to his unending, unendurable pain.

I became involved because the plaintiff was a relative of a partner in the law firm the defendant corporation usually retained to defend lawsuits filed against them. Due to the apparent conflict of interest, the partner recommended that I represent the corporation. In planning my defense of the lawsuit, I had to completely change my thinking about the elements of the case and how to defend my corporate client. The plaintiff was seeking millions of dollars in damages.

The facts of the case developed through the depositions and written documents established that my client had submitted a bid to remove an existing floor in the dealership's service department and replace it with our proprietary flooring system. The plaintiff's counsel was a well-known personal injury trial lawyer who had won dozens of million dollar cases, and his preparation of the case was meticulous, persuasive, and impressive.

The plaintiff had been a certified mechanic with many years of experience at this dealership. His workstation was in one of the bays in the colossal service department next to the car wash station. He kept his tools in his own locked, multi-drawer, red storage box at the far end of the bay. The bay had a lift to raise the vehicles he would work on, and he was responsible for cleaning his work area at the end of his shift. The cleaning included sweeping the entire bay to remove any fallen debris so the oncoming mechanic would have a clean, well-swept service bay to work in.

The plaintiff's injuries occurred when he slipped and fell on the floor surface my client had installed. He claimed the floor was removed and resurfaced with grit in the mixture, and he alleged that our workers did not spread the grit evenly across the floor when installing the floor. According to him, this defective installation left extremely slippery areas in his work bay. He slipped on one of the smooth areas that had no grit.

In Illinois, when a person is injured on the job, and the injury arose out of and during their employment, they can file a claim for their work injury and collect for the nature and extent of their injuries from their employer's workers' compensation carrier.

If a third party participated in causing the work injury, the employee may also file a claim against that third party. If successful, the employee can collect damages from the third party. If that claim is successful, the workers' compensation insurance carrier is entitled to recoup some of the workers' compensation benefits it had paid.

The plaintiff had already collected over a quarter million dollars from the workers' compensation claim and sought much more from my client.

The case was scheduled for a jury trial. The plaintiff presented his case, which was a new experience for me. As the attorney representing the defendant for the first time in my career, I had to sit there for three days while the plaintiff's attorney meticulously constructed a case that covered every conceivable aspect of liability or fault on the part of my client, including the plaintiff's description of the surface of his work bay, the slippery areas of the bay, and his observations of the service department.

He also described his debilitating injuries. He had to give up the SAE-certified mechanical work he had performed his entire career and emphasized how much money he lost by changing job duties. Instead of working on the car's mechanical problems, he was replacing air-conditioning equipment, preparing vehicles for delivery, cleaning and washing the cars sold, filling them with gas, and doing a five-mile test drive. I envied the plaintiff's attorney's presentation and had to snap out of my adoration to remember what my task was for my client.

After the plaintiff finished testifying, I was able to cross-examine the plaintiff. I had him describe the physical layout of the work bay. He explained how the floor had been installed about two years before his accident. He was aware that there were smooth areas and gritty areas. He usually avoided slippery spots, but just before his fall, on the occasion of his incident, he wasn't paying attention to the floor while sweeping it clean. He admitted that the wash bay was adjacent to his work area, and occasionally, soapy water would drain into his work area, but not on the day of his fall. He also admitted that in his new assignment, removing and replacing air conditioner compressors required him to bend into the engine compartment of the cars assigned to him. He often had to lift the AC compressor from the engine compartment; each unit weighed about fifty pounds. The plaintiff also mentioned that his back ached from the bending required to work on the air-conditioning units at the end of every day.

I asked him about his cleaning activities. He claimed he used a twenty-four-inch push broom, which he used to sweep and clean the bay. He testified that for the two or more years since our installation, he swept the entire bay clean and never noticed any slippery area when he swept the floor. I took out a similar broom I had brought to the trial and had the plaintiff agree that it was like the one he used. I started to mimic the sweeping motion in the middle of the courtroom while asking him if he had ever noticed, during the sweeping motion, that the broom slipped over a smooth or slippery spot. He testified that he never saw such a thing. Then I put my broom away. I asked a few questions about his back condition and what aggravated it, and he confirmed that he had volunteered to do the air-conditioning replacements because he made more money doing that than the mechanical work. At the end of a workday, his back was in pain and has been like that since his fall. He admitted he never notified our company of any condition on the floor which concerned him.

It was then my turn to call my witness from the floor installer. He testified about his job duties and responsibilities, the bidding process in selling a new floor surface, his familiarity with the installation, and his knowledge of the type of surface the dealership purchased. He admitted that the dealership wanted grit in the floors so vehicles and workers wouldn't slip around. He took out a picture of the floor that had been installed and described, in detail, how the floor surface was installed. He explained that the previously existing floor surface was removed entirely. Once that's been done, the concrete is prepared with a primer. Then, a layer of grit is spread evenly across the primed area, and a machine is calibrated to distribute the grit precisely and uniformly. After the grit is laid, a third layer, a sealer, is spread over the grit, like an OREO™ cookie. He explained that the floor couldn't have an exposed layer of grit, especially in a car dealer service department, because, he said, the oil and grease would adhere to the grit, preventing it from being adequately cleaned. He also provided testimony that our company had installed hundreds of car dealership floors without a single incident or injury.

In my view, the plaintiff's case had been shattered. As partial as I was, I believed their theory was a fiction that exposed grit, or the lack thereof, as the cause of the plaintiff's fall. It was just as likely the drainage from the wash station next to him caused the slippery condition. Moreover, in my closing argument, I asked what type of person with an operated back in daily disabling pain would volunteer to work under the hood of a car eight hours a day, repairing and replacing air conditioning units.

I had a high level of anxiety when the proofs were closed, not knowing if my presentation of the defense was persuasive. When they came out of the jury room about two hours later, the verdict against my client was a resounding "not guilty." My client was ecstatic. I had never felt such relief at the end of any case I tried.

Speeding on the Expressway:

In Illinois, the automobile insurance industry has been populated by various carriers who run the gamut of very high-quality companies that operate their businesses with integrity and competence to nonstandard carriers that skimp on service and dispute everything. Generally, high-quality companies investigate and pay legitimate claims promptly and fairly. A lawsuit is filed if a claim cannot be resolved between the claimant and the carrier. Those companies hire professional, ethical law firms to defend their insureds.

On the contrary, nonstandard carriers issue minimum liability limit policies and charge very high premiums, primarily to high-risk drivers. Consumers who purchase those policies account for the highest incidents of complaints from their insureds. Some companies conduct their business to frustrate their very customers.

At one time, I represented a client who was in a car crash and who happened to be a former employee of one of the nonstandard carriers. While handling her case, we'd had several conversations about her former job, and she told me she had been the receptionist for one of those companies. She told me her "training" to handle the receptionist desk was to pick up the telephone to answer the call after no less than four to five rings. Then her response to the caller was, "—— Insurance. Please hold." She then placed the caller on "hold" for at least five minutes. Managers in the company told her that the company had done studies, which indicated that after five minutes, most callers would hang up and not call again. That was their business model and general method of operation.

My experience with nonstandard carriers exposed me to those business practices at the claim stage, where you could never reach a claims adjuster. If you did contact them through mailing in the claim documents, their attitude was either an outright denial or an offer so low that your only alternative was to file a lawsuit.

After filing lawsuits, the carrier's law firms retained to "represent" the alleged at-fault insured driver and adopted the same negative attitude, denying and delaying the proceedings at every turn. Unfortunately for one of my clients, she was struck by a vehicle covered by one of those nonstandard carriers. As I expected, we went through the whole litigation process of pleading, document discovery, and depositions of the parties. The case was eventually set for arbitration.

Our county has an arbitration system where cases of a specific value are arbitrated before two or three arbitrators. The arbitrators were usually drawn from a pool of experienced personal injury attorneys who would hear the evidence in the case and issue an award. The nonstandard carriers routinely rejected arbitration awards, further delaying the eventual outcome. After rejection and fee payment, the case would be returned to the courthouse and set for a full-blown jury trial.

In my experience, the only arbitration awards nonstandard carriers did not reject were those they won. That was generally true, except in one case, where, whether intentionally or in error, an attorney for a nonstandard carrier was so locked into rejecting arbitration awards that they paid the rejection fee and rejected an award in their client's favor.

My most memorable case with a nonstandard carrier involved a client struck from behind while traveling eastbound along the Eisenhower Expressway. He was hit from behind as he approached the old Chicago Post Office in Chicago, near the eastern end of the Eisenhower Expressway. That road runs through a tunnel cut through the post office toward Lake Michigan. My client was driving at fifty miles per hour, about a hundred yards from the post office, when another struck his vehicle. The collision caused significant damage to my client's car and injured him.

We filed a lawsuit against the driver, who was defended by the nonstandard carrier's law firm, which engaged in all the usual shenanigans, delays, and denials throughout the process. Eventually, the case was set for arbitration, and my client and I prepared for the hearing.

At the appointed time and place, we appeared, ready for anything. The arbitrations are conducted in a conference room with a T-shaped table. The arbitrators sit at one end of T, and the litigants sit on either side of the adjoining conference table. The defendant appeared with an attorney from one of the usual suspect defense firms. When the hearing began, I gave a short opening statement regarding what I expected the evidence to prove and what damages we sought. The defendant's attorney waived giving an opening statement. My client was sworn in, and I began my questioning. I asked him about himself and his health condition before the collision date. I had him discuss the state of his vehicle before and after the collision. I wondered what travel lane he was in, his speed, his direction of travel, and how the crash occurred. He said he was in the left lane, about a hundred yards from the post office tunnel, and traveling about fifty miles per hour when, suddenly and violently, he was hit from behind, pushing his vehicle into the guardrail. I inquired about his injuries. He told of his pain and how he was transported to the hospital in an ambulance. He described his injuries, his treatment in the emergency department, and his follow-up care. I had him identify pictures of his vehicle, which showed extensive damage to the rear and front after he was hit and struck the guardrails. He testified about the medical bills and how he experienced pain and discomfort for months following his treatment. Then, I rested my case.

It was the defense counsel's chance to cross-examine the plaintiff. The defendant's attorney was a relatively young associate. He had a yellow legal pad containing the notes and questions he intended to present during his cross-examination. He stood very ceremoniously as he started to question my client. Usually, everyone sat through the hearings. He began his questioning. His demeanor was very aggressive, and his voice was louder than necessary, considering the size of the room.

"You testified earlier [it was about eight minutes], Mr. [Plaintiff], that you were eastbound, traveling in the left-hand lane on the Eisenhower, about one hundred yards from the entry to the post office tunnel. Is that correct?"

My client answered, "Yes."

"You also testified you were going FIFTY [emphasis on fifty] miles per hour. Is that correct?"

"Yes, that's correct."

"I will now show you a photograph of that exact location, Mr. [Plaintiff], one hundred yards from the tunnel entrance to the post office." He presented a photograph of the scene to my client.

"Do you recognize that photograph?" He asked. "Yes, I do".

"Is that a photograph of the area you were in just before the collision?"

"Yes," he answered.

"Now, having seen the photograph, you are aware, are you not? The speed limit at that location is FORTY-FIVE miles per hour. Is that correct?"

My client said, "Yes."

"So, Mr. [Plaintiff], if you were going fifty miles per hour, you were speeding, correct?"

"I guess so," my client admitted.

"No further questions," he said, and with a self-satisfying and unmistakable touch of arrogance in his voice, he ceremoniously sat down.

To say I was astonished at this juncture is an understatement of my trial experience. I remained in my seat and asked to call the defendant a "hostile witness." Under the rules, I could call the defendant a witness in my client's case. He was sworn in under oath. "Mr. [Defendant], this collision occurred about one hundred yards from the entry to the post office tunnel, correct?"

"Yes," he answered.

"And you heard my client testify that he was going fifty miles per hour when your car struck his, correct?"

"Yes."

"So, if your car hit my client while he was moving at fifty miles per hour, you must have been going much faster than fifty to overtake and strike him, correct?"

"I guess so," he offered.

"I have no further questions."

We received a very reasonable, unanimous award, which was not rejected by the defense.

Teen Shoplifter Suspect:

Gang warfare is rampant in every village, town, and city. Random violence threatens everyone: shoppers in stores and malls, innocent bystanders, worshippers, people sitting in their homes, grocery clerks, clergy, and bar patrons. Things can become incendiary at the slightest insult; the flash of a gang sign, the wrong color apparel, and tattoos are all causes of gun violence and mayhem.

My involvement with that stark reality came from two teenage freshmen high school students who confronted each other while walking home on a public street. A gang sign was flashed, a threat and an insult to the other boy involved, who recognized the hostile gesture and fled the scene for safety. That began a horror scene for my client's uninvolved son, who did not know about the confrontation.

My client's son was a loss prevention employee in a store near the incident. He was hired to walk around the store and observe the shoppers. If they looked suspicious or were seen trying to steal merchandise it was his job to detain them for the store manager, who would summon the police.

When the insulted, fifteen-year-old, threatened rival gang

member removed himself from the confrontation, he did what any other self-respecting teenage gang member would do in that situation in this day and age: he ran home to retrieve his handgun. Then he called some of his gang buddies, met up with them, and, while fully armed, went looking for the offending gang sign flasher.

At one point, the three-armed hoodlums spotted the offending sign flasher and chased him into the store where my client's son was working. My client's son was eighteen, an EMS candidate, and a future fireman. He was walking through aisles, keeping an eye on the shoppers.

Meanwhile, the armed rivals approached one another in the store, and the insulted, armed teenager displayed his gun in a threatening manner. Someone yelled, and the gun-totter started to run out of the store, concealing the gun in his jacket and behaving like he had stolen merchandise.

My client's son, unaware of the events involving the gang sign incident, assuming this was a shoplifter, ran after him and got a few steps outside the store in hot pursuit. As he steadily gained on the presumed offender, he yelled for him to stop. At that point, the teenager stopped, turned around, pulled out the gun, and shot my client's son three times, killing him.

He was my client's only child. Her son was the apple of her eye. He was an outstanding student, an active churchgoer, her helping hand around the house, and an all-around great young man working to provide the income he and his mom needed to get by. His mother hired me to sue the store, the security service for the store, and the shooter. The shooter was arrested, charged as an adult, tried, and convicted to serve sixty years in prison. My challenge was to prove the store and the security guard service had noticed gang activity around their store, and they both had a duty to my client's son to prevent the intentional shooting and his getting killed.

The store's attorneys and security guard services aggressively defended our action. They claimed it was the fault of my client's son for chasing the gunman, that they had no duty for the intentional shooting, and that their store and security personnel had no notice that any gang activity occurred in the store or parking lot. They retained a highly professional store security expert from the West Coast who had published and testified to the proper procedures for stores to operate safely and securely.

In discovery, they produced his lengthy résumé, which included numerous articles he'd written on mall security. I researched the issues as best I could. When I received the expert's résumé, I learned that there was one publication in the United States with all his published works. They were all in stock on the shelves of an Illinois University, out on the western edge of the state, about two hundred miles from Chicago. One bright morning, I headed to the school, found the publications, and copied all the expert articles to prepare for my cross-examination.

The articles were an encyclopedia of store and shopping mall security operations. Those ranged from the project's design to fencing requirements, reducing entry points, staffing security personnel, removing gang signs that marked the gang turf, video surveillance equipment, metal detection equipment at entry points, reducing entry and access locations for the stores, and record keeping.

After we rested our case against the store and security company, the defense called their expert witness for his testimony, and predictably, he testified that he examined the store and the security procedures and that the defendant companies complied with the standards in the industry. He testified that there was no conceivable way the defendants could have anticipated or predicted the presence of the shooter or prevented the events that led to the death of my client's son. The defense rested, and it was time for me to cross-examine the expert about his opinions.

I started by having the expert identify his education,

experience, and familiarity with the shopping center. He confirmed that he had written and published articles supporting his expertise and opinions in this case. I quoted portions of the articles he wrote directly from his writings. The first was a laundry list he'd prepared of how to establish a safe environment and how removing gang signs was important. Then, I showed him photographs of the gang signs and slogans painted outside the stores and inside the bathroom walls and stalls.

He had written that perimeter fencing would be an essential security measure, so I showed him photographs of the open parking lot with no fencing. He recommended that the staffing of officers be a certain number for a certain amount of square footage of retail space, which was less than this store had, which was a blatant violation of his rules.

I walked him through each item in the expert's published list. The defendant's property hadn't followed any of his recommendations. In essence, their expert became my most valuable witness at the trial.

During the redirect examination, both defense counsels were shaken. They asked the expert about when he had published those articles and where they were located. He proclaimed that there was one repository for those articles at the university I had visited to retrieve and copy them. They rested.

My closing argument was the most difficult I had ever given. Some jurors openly wept when I asked how much money could compensate this mother who had lost her treasure. Even I teared up a little.

After the verdict in our favor, the defense attorneys told me that my cross-examination of their witness was the best cross of any witness they had ever seen. That proved to me preparation was the key, no matter how far you may have to go to get it.

Court of Claims

In many states, laws prevent a person from suing the government. Immunities exempt the government from negligent acts of its authorized executives and officials. In Illinois, a law established a Court of Claims in which claims against the state could be filed and presented to that court. The state establishes a system; the hearing officers are selected and paid, and the defense attorneys are state employees. The law limits the damages a claimant might obtain for any incident. The one exception to the damage cap raises the limit of recoverable damages if a claim arose from or involved a motor vehicle, in which case, there is no limitation on damages.

    The case referred to me involved the death of a young man who had suffered an electrocution injury. The victim was about to end his prison term and was in the last few months of a criminal conviction in a downstate prison. He had good behavior credits and was allowed certain privileges in and around the prison. One of his tasks was assisting a work crew in painting the guard towers on a perimeter road outside the prison gates. The crew was utilizing a pole scaffold to reach the top of the guard tower, and the prisoner (later, the deceased victim) and a guard were using a tractor to pull the scaffold along the road surrounding the prison. There was a high-tension power line along one leg of the perimeter road. The crew had attached the scaffold to the tractor with a chain, and the corrections officer drove the tractor to move the scaffold. The prisoner I represented guided the tower being pulled by the tractor. As the scaffold approached the building, the current in the power line arced and struck the scaffold, seeking a ground, and hit the prisoner, causing his gruesome death. The current melted the tires of the tractor and burned the prisoner. He died instantly.

We filed a claim in the court of claims for the death of our client. In our pleadings, we sought a finding by the presiding judge to declare that the damage cap in the act did not apply. We argued the incident involved a tractor. To my mind, and from all rational analysis, the tractor was a motor vehicle. It had a motor, a steering wheel, and four tires. We filed briefs for our client's estate, and the state filed its response. Eventually, the case and our arguments came up for a hearing before the presiding judge. We provided photographs taken by the guards, showing the towers, the tractor, the melted tires, and our client's smoking, deceased and damaged body.

Months have elapsed with no decision. In my experience, that wasn't unusual. Status hearings were held once a year for the court of claims, and we were already in year 4 of the litigation. When we finally received the decision, I tore open the envelope, fully expecting our argument to prevail and placing no limit on the damages we could claim. I had estimated the value of the case to be in the millions, considering the vile nature of the injuries, and other than his previous behavior that had landed him in prison, he was a model prisoner. To my and the family's dismay and disappointment, the judge ruled that a tractor was not a motor vehicle. Within a few weeks, a payment of $100,000 was tendered to the estate, and we closed the case.

Cutting Corners

I had a client who suffered severe fracture injuries to both hips. He had to undergo surgery and months of rehabilitation. When I met to discuss his claim, he told me he was a warehouse factory worker operating a forklift machine. At the end of his shift, he would park his forklift in an area with several bays. The forklifts were driven into a bay and recharged for the next day's work. He was walking across one of the bays when a coworker driving one of the forklifts couldn't stop his vehicle and ran into my client, crushing him against a wall and fracturing his hips.

I immediately considered filing a claim with the Illinois Workers' Compensation Commission. The incident occurred during the course and scope of his work, arose out of employment, and was caused by a coworker. You can't sue a co-employee in worker compensation actions if they cause your injury. The facts of the case were straightforward, and I was confident we'd recover a sizable settlement of the claim.

The workers' compensation claim arose from a malfunction of the forklift, which could be a separate source of recovery if we could prove the device malfunctioned. So, I investigated the machine, its manufacture, and its operation.

Suppose a product fails due to a defect in its design, manufacture, maintenance, or operational characteristics, and it could be proven that the defect existed when it left the manufacturer. In that case, a claim can be made against the designer, manufacturer, installer, or service provider. These cases are third-party recoveries.

Considering the seriousness of the injuries, I believe it would be well worth the time and expense of investigating and pursuing a third-party claim against the forklift company. In that regard, if we were to recover, my client's employer or their worker's compensation insurer would be entitled to recoup a percentage of the money it paid my client from his work injury recovery.

My investigation revealed that the forklift manufacturer was located in eastern Iowa, near the Illinois border. Online sources produced images of the forklift, from design schematics to operations. I obtained a copy of the instruction manuals and pored through them to establish a theory of what had occurred. I also searched for similar models of forklift machines to become informed about their products.

I also checked the company's personnel, the owner's experience, and the company designers, engineers, assembly staff, and instructors.

After filing suit, I started the discovery process. I issued written questions and requests for documents from the company and thoroughly reviewed the materials. Then, I scheduled some of the sworn statements of the company's principals, starting with the lead engineer who designed the forklift involved in my client's case.

My client showed me some photographs of the warehouse where he worked. The warehouse was set up with stacks of storage shelves, like the ones you see in big-box stores nationwide. The aisles were barely wide enough for the forklift to maneuver through.

I scheduled the depositions to start with the chief engineer as the first witness. I reviewed his résumé for his education, training, degrees, experience, and the myriad issues that went into the forklift's design.

His résumé and my questioning revealed that the gentleman was not an engineer. He'd been a warehouse worker who was familiar with using a forklift. He had operated forklifts from other manufacturers and studied those designs. When the company decided to manufacture their forklifts during his years there, he was reluctant to plagiarize other manufacturer's designs for fear of copyright infringement, so he modified the operational controls.

Other manufacturers had design features with thumb activation and toggle switches on the handlebars used to steer the forklift. The handlebars on the different vehicles did not extend beyond the side of the forklift. He modified the handlebars by placing the toggle switches into groves along the handlebar. In his design, the handlebars on the forklifts in their manufacture would extend beyond the side of the forklift's body. Because of the narrow aisles, from time to time, when the operators drove the forklifts through the narrow stacks of shelves, the handlebar would strike the metal stacks and close the groove where the thumb toggle switch was located, jamming the switch in the on position, making it impossible to stop the forklift. That happened when my client's coworker couldn't stop his vehicle before entering the parking bay where he was walking.

When the "engineer's" testimony ended, the company attorney asked me not to leave and remain in the conference room. I waited there while the executives had a closed-door meeting. Within a very short time, he returned with an offer we couldn't refuse. My client was ecstatic with the outcome. Preparation was the key to a successful result.

Missed the Mark

Whenever a person is injured in a work-related incident, especially when the injury is severe, I usually ask questions of my clients to determine if the cause of the accident was a third party's involvement, whether it be a motorist who caused a work-related collision, a defect on the premises, or a defective product.

One case I was handling involved a young, single man who sustained a very severe head injury. He worked for a company that was engaged in manufacturing that utilized cutting tools. The tool he was using was in the shape of a standard electric drill. It had a motor in a housing to which circular cutting discs were attached. His job was to place a cutting disc on the machine, and then, holding the machine by hand, he would cut the metal objects the company manufactured. He wore gloves, a "face shield" (a little more than a headband with a clear piece of plastic, and knee pads.

He was given a cutting project in the usual and customary course of a day's work. He placed a disc on the cutting tool and started the job. In a few minutes, the blade exploded, shattered, flew off the machine, cut through the face shield, and severed his face across his nose and cheek. He was rushed to the hospital, had multiple surgeries, and months of rehabilitation to repair his nose and face, leaving horrible scars. He became depressed and an alcoholic.

The work injury claim was indefensible. We received total compensation for the lost time from work, psychological counseling, and awards for the injury and disfigurement. I was very involved with this client and empathized with his plight. He'd had a girlfriend who rejected him; he could not visit his old hangouts; he abandoned his friends, and, of all things bizarre, he confided in me all his demons. I was involved as his attorney, but I felt more like a friendly shoulder to rely on.

So, I pursued a third-party case regarding this accident. I started with the machine and the discs. With the workers' compensation carrier's representative, I visited the workplace. I took pictures of the tool, the discs, and the labels affixed to them. I immediately noticed that the label on the device itself had markings that had worn away with use. I couldn't read the details other than those of the manufacturer. I obtained pamphlets and brochures about cutting tools and discs used in the industry. I went to a local tool supply store and took photographs of the labels on similar machines.

I developed a theory of recovery against the tool manufacturer and filed a lawsuit on behalf of my client. The allegations in the complaint were based on our argument that the machine itself was not a defective product. All its parts, components, and operations were appropriate. However, I theorized and pled that the defect arose from not having the operational characteristics visible and not being subject to the anticipated wear and tear in the workplace. The information, the model number, and the serial number had worn off. The most essential item that had disappeared was the rotational speed of the cutter. The sample I found of like shape and style had a speed of ten thousand rotations per minute. The sample cutters had those items etched into the label so they could not be obliterated with ordinary use. My client's cutting blades had maximum rotational cutting speeds of five thousand revolutions per minute. By not knowing the machine's speed and the cutting disc's speed tolerance, my client was subject to a disastrous outcome. The disparity and lack of the information necessary to select an appropriate disc for that machine caused this horrible incident and injuries. I claimed that the failure to properly warn potential users was a defect present when the device left the manufacturer.

We collected from the machine manufacturer, settled with the workers' compensation carrier, and enrolled our client in a rehabilitation program. After undergoing several cosmetic procedures, he could continue with his life.

Missing Humidifier:

A lawyer should not get involved in family legal issues. A matter of principles is not a prudent basis for litigation. The cost of litigating a dispute can run well above the argument's value. A relative bought a condominium apartment. I wasn't involved in the closing. Part of the transaction involved the seller certifying that all the equipment, fixtures, and appliances in the unit were in "good working order" at the time of the sale.

The closing occurred, and the buyers moved in. They checked all the appliances, and everything was in working order except for minor issues.

However, when they attempted to turn on the humidifier in a separate room adjacent to the residence, they discovered it was not working. It wasn't working, and the power wires connected to the humidifier weren't even there. The representation that the humidifier was in good working order was false.

I was requested to write a letter to the sellers advising them of the apparent misrepresentation and sending them an estimate for a replacement humidifier. My clients had an HVAC engineer examine the nonfunctioning unit and inform them that their type of humidifier was no longer manufactured and that replacement parts weren't available.

The sellers ignored my letter and refused to respond. They were so obviously responsible for replacing the humidifier that I advised my relatives to file a lawsuit. We prepared the suit and issued a summons against the sellers, which they deliberately tried to avoid accepting. I had to retain a particular process server who tracked them down. Then, they demanded their real estate closing attorney represent them. He wasn't a litigator and knew very little about the process. This was going to be the most straightforward trial I had ever presented. The contract, the representation, and the photographs we had of the broken humidifier were all admissible into evidence, so I prepared a document and filed it with the court to conduct an immediate trial. After a defense request for a delay, which the court reluctantly allowed, we were set for trial. At trial, facing an inevitable loss, the sellers offered the cost of the new humidifier and our court fees and costs in full. The story's moral is never to underestimate the wrath of an attorney scorned.

Anti-rotational Braces:

I represented a woman who came into my office in crutches with a brace that ran from her mid-thigh to her left foot. The brace had metal flanges with Velcro straps, and her leg was immovable. She described how she was injured. She was a competitive skier, and in training for a position on a team, she wanted to make, with a view toward Olympic participation. She had a knee injury many years before, had surgery, and was fitted with an "anti-rotational" brace. She had healed from the previous surgery through lengthy, extensive, and exhaustive knee rehabilitation. She'd recently returned to skiing, eventually moving into competitive skiing again. She had been fitted with a new anti-rotational brace. The brace's design was to prevent her knee and leg from rotating while skiing. She went to make a turn in a slalom event, the brace rotated, her knee didn't, and she had a second injury to the same leg, never to ski again. Her brace was custom-made, molded to her leg, and still failed.

The manufacturer's design needed to be thoroughly tested under real-world conditions, and the stresses imposed by skiing maneuvers required to be improved.

ANTI-ROTATIONAL BRACES:

The product manufacturer stood firm on their denial after I notified them of her incident, but, faced with a trial, a credible witness, enormous medical expenses, and the two failures, eventually, we worked out a settlement.

The Centerline

A serious collision occurred between a vehicle and a motorcycle in rural DuPage County on a busy, rural highway. I did not routinely practice in DuPage County and was unfamiliar with the judge or prosecutor. My female client was a passenger on the motorcycle and was seriously injured in the crash. She had multiple surgeries for leg fractures and muscle injuries, which required months of therapy and rehabilitation. The girl's family retained me to represent her. Her boyfriend was the motorcycle's driver, and he'd been charged with driving over the center line and allegedly driving while intoxicated. The girl swore her boyfriend was not drunk and never crossed the center line. They were always in their lane of travel.

The driver of the car that hit them was also charged with intoxicated driving. We had placed the car driver's insurance carrier on notice of my client's claim, and to my surprise, when the traffic court hearing occurred, I noticed the insurance carrier's attorney was present in the courtroom. I knew him from cases I had previously litigated with him.

He was known to the prosecutor, and I noticed they were

having a lengthy conversation before the two driving charges were called for trial.

The prosecutor informed the presiding judge that they were dropping the intoxicated driving charges against the car driver and only prosecuting the motorcycle-driving boyfriend.

In civil or criminal litigation, the party making the claim has a burden of proof. In civil cases, the burden on the claimant is to prove their claim is more probably valid than not true. In criminal cases, the burden for the prosecution is to prove their case beyond a reasonable doubt. The prosecution had to prove the motorcycle driver (boyfriend) was intoxicated above a certain blood alcohol level and that he crossed the center line and struck the motor vehicle. The female prosecutor called the car driver to testify. He was sworn under oath and testified, in summary, and not verbatim, that he was driving along the highway, it was at night, there wasn't street lighting in the area, and he was unfamiliar with the road. He was traveling around fifty miles per hour. As he came up to the site where the collision eventually occurred, the headlight from the motorcycle affected his ability to see the road markings, and the crash occurred. He couldn't testify truthfully whether the motorcycle crossed the centerline.

Then, I was given the right to cross-examine the car driver, knowing that the prosecutor had dropped the intoxication claim. I asked the driver where he'd been that night, and he admitted he was out with friends at a bar, drinking and watching television. He was tired and left to drive home. He was unfamiliar with the road and could not be sure if he was still in his travel lane when the collision occurred.

He never saw the motorcycle in his travel lane and could not say if the bike crossed the centerline.

The prosecutor then called the investigating police officer to testify. He was sworn in and testified about his education, experience, licensure, and training as a police officer. He testified about his familiarity with the investigation of car crashes and the preparation of reports to be clear, truthful, and accurate.

He swore he was the investigating officer for the collision and wrote the incident report. The report was offered and admitted into evidence.

He continued to say he spoke with both the car and motorcycle drivers. He never noticed any smell of alcohol on the motorcycle operator, so he charged him with driving under the influence anyway. The motorcycle was found at or near the center line of the roadway. The debris field from the crash was in the motorcycle's lane of travel, so he gave the opinion that the collision was in the motorcycle's lane. He never had the motorcycle operator do a field sobriety test.

With that, I rested. The judge asked if I wished to call any witnesses. Had I not been a litigator or recognized the tactic of the prosecutor and defendant's attorney in only going after the motorcycle operator, I might have had the urge to call him as a witness. However, I realized that the criminal defendant, the motorcycle operator in this case, need not present a defense. The prosecution had not met the high burden of proving intoxication or that the motorcycle crossed the centerline beyond a reasonable doubt. I rested my case without the boyfriend's testimony.

The judge promptly ruled in our favor, and the criminal case for intoxication and crossing the center line was dismissed. During the traffic trial, the defense attorney listened intently to all the testimony and was surprised that I rested my case without calling any witnesses. I'm sure he was there to obtain testimony against the motorcycle operator, which he could use to defend the passenger's civil suit. The motorcycle driver was acquitted of my motion to dismiss. I had beaten the case without submitting him to sworn testimony. The civil defense attorney approached me and said my strategy and cross-examination were masterful. I obtained a sworn affidavit from the defendant's mouth about intoxication and confusion, and the officer's testimony was conclusive on who crossed the center line, all of which would serve my client well in the civil suit. Shortly after the trial and some discussion with the insurance attorney, we settled the passenger's injury case.

Jury Duty

Contrary to widespread belief, many good citizens accept the opportunity to serve on a jury as their civic duty. Judges always point out how precious the right to serve on a jury is and how other countries don't allow their citizens to serve. It is a fascinating experience, so I urge everyone to do it once they're called. Just as many resent being called to serve and try to avoid service.

In the past, lawyers, judges, and other professionals were exempt from jury service, but that is no longer true. Everyone is eligible to be called and serve.

I received a notice to serve on jury duty and appeared in our local courthouse, where a particular sequestered holding area was set up for potential jurors. When a jury case was called for a civil or criminal trial, the judge would request the Sheriff to go to the holding area and bring an array of potential jurors to a courtroom. I was in an array and called to the presiding judge's courtroom to be questioned about our qualifications to serve as unbiased, totally neutral jurors.

When I was called for jury duty, I'd already been practicing law for several years and had appeared before the judge hearing the case many times. The judge had a eputation for being stern and no-nonsense. He could be spontaneous and direct and would interrupt an argument midsentence if he didn't like the presentation.

The judge nodded and acknowledged me as I entered the room. I sat in the gallery at the back of the courtroom. The bailiff called everyone's attention to open the proceedings, and the judge entered very ceremoniously. Everyone rose and was sworn in under oath.

"Do you swear and affirm that you shall well and truly answer all questions the court and counsel put to you? If you do, say 'I will.'" Everyone responded.

The judge introduced himself and gave preliminary comments about himself, the court, and a brief case summary. He mentioned that the case would take about three days to complete and asked if they knew any of the parties or counsel. A few people raised their hands, and the judge questioned who they knew. He moved to me as I had raised my hands well.

"State your name," he said. I did.

"Who do you know?" he inquired.

"Well, Your Honor," I started, "I know the plaintiff's attorney; I know the defendant's attorney; I have a pending case with the defense attorney, which is set before you next week; and I know the defendant's doctor, who is an expert in one of my cases." I stood up to leave when the judge said, "Where do you think you're going?" I said, "Well, Judge, considering I know everyone in the case, I figured no one was going to pick me for this jury."

"Sit down," said the judge very sternly.

The gist of that conversation was that if I were selected to be on the jury after he questioned me, he would make one of the attorneys use a peremptory challenge to kick me off the jury and not sit to reach a verdict. I sat down.

The judge asked if anyone else knew any of the parties or the attorneys, and a young lady raised her hand, but the judge didn't ask her anything about that. After those preliminary steps, the judge ordered the clerk to say the names of the first twelve jurors selected at random to sit in the courtroom jury box.

The lady who had raised her hand, acknowledging she knew someone, was seated in the first row, the first seat. That seat is notorious. The judge usually asks the most questions of that potential juror to acquaint the other potential jurors with the type of questions they'll be asked. I was seated in the first seat, second row, directly behind the lady juror.

Questioning potential jurors is focused on their qualifications to be fair and impartial. Suppose the judge determines a person will not be fair, unbiased, or some other disqualifying circumstance, e.g., they have a pending case or an illness, or they can't be fair. In that case, the judge can remove them "for cause."

If he believes the potential juror can be fair, the attorneys could ask each juror follow-up questions and utilize challenges to remove them. Usually, if the case involves one plaintiff and one defendant, each side will have five peremptory challenges. There is another reason for the questioning. The judge wants the remainder of the panel to be safe from an errant answer, or he must declare a mistrial and request another array of jurors from the holding area.

The judge began his questioning of juror number 1. I've selected juries in my practice dozens and dozens of times. The attorney can't use the questioning to indoctrinate their theory of the case or subvert the process. So, the questions usually scratch the surface of their education, experience, family, occupation, and litigation experience, if any.

This judge was so intense his questioning of the woman in front of me lasted more than an hour. He went through her entire life history, where she lived as a child, her schools, her work, her driving experience, her medical condition, her biases about sitting on a jury, her litigation experience, and her family history on each topic. It was wild how much detail he went into.

There is a cardinal rule in litigation. Never ask a witness a question that you might not already know the answer. In this case, the judge was shooting from the hip.

Finally, after such a lengthy interrogation, he asked, "I noticed when I asked the jurors if they knew any of the parties or counsel, you raised your hand."

She said, "Yes, I did."

He asked, "Well, who do you know, and under what circumstances?" She said, "Well, about eight years ago, I had some fertility problems and visited with the defendant's doctor." And she gratuitously added, "And he was negligent then, too." The jurors erupted in shock and laughter.

The judge turned bright red.

He trumpeted, "Sheriff, clear the courtroom. I'm declaring a mistrial! "And with that, he stood up and angrily left the bench.

I said, "Lady, I can't thank you enough." Every juror was excused. I was allowed to leave and not called for any other cases.

No Class Action

Class-action litigation is novel. One alleged aggrieved person may have been wronged, and, in theory, the action against the suspected wrongdoer may have harmed a large group of people under similar circumstances. Under that theory, an attorney representing the aggrieved claimant can file an action for themself and all others who have suffered the same way. Those claims are aggressively defended. Usually, the first defense is that the named plaintiff isn't an appropriate class representative. Another argument may be that the lawsuit can't be treated as a class because the purported class members weren't harmed similarly. Such claims are complex, and the expenses to litigate them may be enormous. Usually, notice is required to be given to all of the potential class members. A property owner came to my office with a problem, which might have qualified as a class action. After hearing the details, I agreed to file the lawsuit and pursue the matter.

The claim centered on the insurance premiums paid for liability insurance on his building. The company billed the annual premium, and each month's charge would be deducted from the paid-in premiums. My client had receipts showing all his deposits and each month's payment. He informed me that the company closed its operations but never refunded the unused portion of the premium to him, and it was likely they weren't returned to any of the other insureds.

I filed the class-action lawsuit and had the Sheriff serve the lawsuit on the insurance carrier. Within the week, an attorney from a nationally known law firm called my office. He wanted to set up a meeting to discuss the complaint. My client and I agreed, figuring it would be advantageous to get the insurance company involved early in the case before they filed pleadings and engaged in what would likely be extensive, time-consuming, and costly litigation.

Two attorneys appeared at my office a week later and exchanged pleasantries. We noticed they each had a briefcase, which wasn't necessarily unusual. When we sat down for the meeting, the lead attorney said, "We've been waiting for your lawsuit for months." I was surprised by his statement. "What do you mean?" I asked.

"When the company closed its doors, we had all these policyholders, but none came forward to claim the refund of their premiums. Some were so small that the insured policyholder probably ignored the balance due, but your client had almost a year's premium due."

With that, he opened his briefcase and removed a bound volume with every insured's name, address, policy number, and the amount of premium to be reimbursed. He handed me a binder and said, "Look this over and let us know if you agree with the numbers. We'll meet again in a week to discuss the method of handling the reimbursements and your fee and costs."

They left the office, and our stunned expressions.

This had to be the most straightforward class action in history.

We tallied all the premiums and added them up. Their additional skills needed to be more questionable. They had listed premiums that tallied thousands less than the total refunds due. We produced a correct, itemized list, assessed a reasonable fee for our services and filing costs, and within a few weeks, a check was sent to us to distribute to our client and each policyholder. Then, the funds were deposited and distributed to the class members. The case was over before it began.

Head-On Crash, Smart Jury:

One of the most fascinating aspects of practicing law has been my astonishment at the convergence of all the elements that go into a litigated matter. The facts of the case, the law applicable to it, the personalities of the parties and the attorneys, and how they all collide in the courtroom create stories that stay with you forever. It has very little to do with winning or losing. You can have a "perfect" case on the facts, and the law may stop you in your effort. You can have a problematic fact situation, but the law provides an avenue for victory. Even the slightest case can bear witness to some remarkable outcomes. In some instances, the enormity of the injury compels a lawyer to try to achieve a result.

Such was the case with a head-on motor vehicle crash between two vehicles on Chicago Street. The facts were simple enough. A car was heading southbound along the road, hit a foot-deep pothole, went out of control, crossed the center line, and struck my clients' northbound vehicle, injuring the driver and a passenger. They hired me to represent them for their injuries.

As a fundamental premise, municipalities are the owners of the common ways. The government and its departments will maintain roads, bridges, and sidewalks. Usually, if repair work is to be done by a municipality, it issues requests for bids, and contractors submit proposals for the work. The lowest bidder usually gets the job, and the contractor posts a bond or insurance policy that the work will be done expeditiously, competently, and entirely according to approved plans. The municipality issuing the work order inspects the work at each stage. Once approved and the work is complete, the municipality sends its employees to pave over the excavated, repaired area to the grade level of the street.

Months before my clients' collision, the city issued work orders for plumbing work to be performed in the southbound travel lanes. A plumbing contractor submitted a bid and was awarded the repair of broken pipes below the street. It was issued a permit and performed the work. Once he completed the work, the contractor reported his progress and requested an inspection by a city inspector. The city inspector visited and approved the work. In compliance with the city's rules, the contractor backfilled the hole they had dug to within three inches of the street grade and removed the temporary plate they had placed over the excavation, their work having been completed and approved. After the inspection, the city paving department should have visited the construction site and requested that the paving department fill the area with asphalt. Months went by, and traffic along the roadway had repeatedly struck the backfilled, unpaved hole, creating a depression more than a foot deep in the path of travel.

After the collision and my clients' recovery, we filed a lawsuit against the driver of the southbound vehicle and the city for negligence. The vehicle driver sued the city, and the city filed a cross-suit against the plumbing contractor, claiming it was negligent in performing the work. During the discovery phase, I retrieved the documentation for the plumbing job. I obtained the permit application, the plans, and specifications for the work, the city's work order, the plumbing contractor's plans, the contract, the bids, the award, the bond that had been posted, all the inspection reports, and in particular, the city's authorization issued to the contractor that allowed them to remove the temporary plate after the excavation was backfilled to within three inches of grade. I also received the city's order to its paving department, which was dated weeks after my clients' collision.

One of the discovery methods we use in litigation is the taking of depositions of the parties and the witnesses who will testify at the actual trial. A deposition is a sworn statement where the attorney questions a witness, under oath, to determine their version of what occurred. I took the deposition of the inspector who visited the construction site and authorized the plumbing contractor to backfill the excavation and remove the plate. I confirmed that he approved the plumbing contractor and signed the document stating that the contractor needed to remove the plate and receive payment.

I then inquired about the city's process for requesting the paving department to finish their task of paving over the excavation to grade level.

He explained that he would complete his inspection report and mail it to the city's administrative office at City Hall in downtown Chicago. The plumbing work was done in a far south-side district office, where the construction and collision occurred.

He also informed me that those authorizations might sit on some supervisors' desks for a long time. He noted that sometimes, it took months for the supervisor to contact the district office's paving department.

Then, I asked him to view the paving authorization form, dated weeks after the collision. He acknowledged that was the pertinent authorization for that job.

Then I asked where the paving supervisor's desk was in the

district office, and he pointed to his side. "At the desk two feet away from mine," he said.

The witness testimony at the trial of the case revealed all those facts. At the end of all the testimony, each party gave their closing arguments, describing their position on what the evidence has proven to support their case and why the jury should issue a verdict. At that point, the judge usually instructs the jury on the law, reading written instructions to the jury and explaining how they should apply the facts they heard from the witnesses and how to use them to the law to reach their verdict.

After the closing arguments and before reading the jury instructions, the plumbing contractor's counsel asked to be heard, and we all stepped up to the judge's bench. The jury was then returned to a secluded room next to the courtroom.

Outside the jury's presence, the plumbing contractor's attorney presented a written motion, submitting a legal argument requesting the judge to enter an order dismissing his client, the plumbing contractor, as a party to the lawsuit. He argued that there were no facts upon which the contractor could be held liable for creating the defect or causing the collision. The city's documents proved that they had done everything they were legally bound to do. The town submitted some counterarguments, which were unpersuasive, and the presiding judge issued a ruling dismissing the plumbing contractor from the case. Consequently, the jury instructions were modified, removing the claim by the city against the plumbing contractor. The judge and counsel agreed to submit the case for a verdict by and between the plaintiff, the vehicle operator who struck my client's vehicle, and the city, omitting any reference to the plumbing contractor.

However, the ruling created a legal and practical dilemma. Whenever a jury has heard all the evidence and is about the deliberate, if they were informed that the plumbing contractor had been dismissed, they could construe the contractor's

Head-On Crash, Smart Jury:

dismissal as a signal a settlement had been reached, which would be a false message. All the counsel and the judge agreed that he would not disclose the dismissal of the plumbing contractor, and no written verdict form would be submitted as to the issues in the city's lawsuit against the plumbing contractor.

The jury came out of their sequester, and the judge read the jury instructions to them, and then the jury retired to the jury room once again to deliberate their verdict. The jury took all the written instructions and verdict forms for every scenario they could determine. They had forms for verdicts for my client against the driver of the out-of-control vehicle, other forms for my clients against the city or the driver and the city, and defense verdicts. No verdict form applied to the city's case against the plumbing contractor, which made the judge's decision irrelevant. Personal injury lawsuits require juries to deliberate to a unanimous verdict. All twelve jurors must agree and sign the appropriate verdict form.

A few hours later, the jury signaled they had reached a unanimous verdict. The clerk called the attorneys, and we returned to the courtroom. The jurors were ushered into the jury box, and the last juror held a fistful of papers. He was the foreman of the jury. I had reservations about selecting him during jury selection. He was a professional engineer, well-educated, intelligent, and articulate. I was fearful he'd dominate the deliberations or create a one-person jury, which most trial attorneys fear.

The judge asked, "Has the jury reached a verdict?" "Yes, Your Honor," he said. "We have."

"Is it a unanimous verdict?" the judge inquired.

"Yes, Your Honor," he said. "We've reached several verdicts."

"Please read each verdict aloud," the judge said.

The foreman read each verdict regarding the case between my clients, the driver, and the city. Then he said, "Your

Honor, we also reached a verdict on an issue for which we were not given a verdict form."

The judge asked, "Was that additional verdict a unanimous verdict?"

"Yes, Your Honor," he responded.

"Please read that document, Mr. Foreperson," said the judge.

The foreman took a five-by-seven-inch piece of scratch paper he was holding and read it, "We, the jury, find in favor of [the plumbing contractor] and against the City of Chicago." Below that, they had handwritten signature lines, and the printed names of each juror, and each juror had signed their name to the makeshift jury verdict.

After all the congratulatory comments by the judge to the jurors, appreciation for their outstanding service, and laudatory remarks to all the attorneys, the jurors stood around. They asked each of us some questions.

The judge mentioned their creativity in drafting a makeshift jury verdict form and applauded them for their effort in addressing an issue that had yet to be presented. She explained the dismissal order she had entered in the plumbing contractor's favor.

The foreperson stated, "We realized there wasn't a form on the city's claim," he said. "The jury wanted to ensure the city didn't get any relief against the contractor." That was the smartest jury with which I had ever tried a case. Their diligence in addressing all the issues, even those not presented to them, demonstrated the best effort by a jury I had ever experienced.

THE WELL-WORN PATH
TO DISASTER

Young people, especially college students, have a misguided sense of immortality and don't recognize the risks they often take. Diving into a local swimming hole without knowing the depth of the water, speeding down an unknown country road, or climbing rocks or hills without safety lines are threats to their well-being that they don't or won't appreciate.

In many college towns, the popular hangout spots have a flexible and lenient age threshold, further complicating the students' judgment if they are overserved.

I was contacted by a family whose son had been struck and killed by a freight train at his college. They sent me a copy of the police report of the incident, which described in detail, in multiple pages, the result of an escapade the young man was on before it led to his untimely death. The family wanted me to investigate what had occurred to satisfy their curiosity and assuage their guilt over his demise.

I'd never had a visceral reaction to reading a police report before the one they produced. There was the usual narrative of what had occurred and a diagram of the tracks, with descriptive entries, like "shoe," "piece of a foot," "torso," and "leg" strewn over the length of the diagram. It was so morbid and matter-of-fact that it remains in the darkest part of my memory—another reason to respect safe practice near any railroad premises.

The report identified a witness whose name, address, and telephone number were disclosed. I contacted him, and he related what had occurred.

He and his friend, the victim, were in college at a school in Southern Illinois. The college campus was in a small town bisected by railroad tracks. The college was on one side of the tracks, which were in a culvert. The city and its social scene, bars, restaurants, bookstore, and theater were on the other side of the tracks.

To reach the town, the roadway from the college dorms to the city was a half mile south of the school. So, students would have to walk to the road, cross over a bridge over the tracks in the ditch, and then walk to the town. When they finished the night's activities, they had to reverse the route to return to the dorms and a strict curfew. This was inconvenient for the student body.

A fence line along the ditch was on both sides of the tracks. Over time, some unknown person had cut through the fence on both sides, and a pathway was created, which my client's son and his friend, as well as many others, had used as a shortcut from the college to the town and back. The night of the events that led to the death of my client's son, he and his friend had been to town and were headed back to the dorms. The friend was in the lead and was inattentive to an approaching train. It was dark, and they were late, and the friend started to cross the tracks ahead of the train. Seeing this unfolding before him, the client's son realized his friend was in danger, caught like a deer in the headlights. He lunged forward, pushing his friend across the tracks, just as the train approached, which struck and killed the boy. He was nineteen and drinking, and both boys made bad judgments.

The Well-Worn Path to Disaster

The family wanted me to investigate the events, so I undertook the gruesome task of visiting the scene, taking photographs of the area, and retrieving documents about the postmortem investigation. I found the fence and photographed it, along with the apparent pathway the boys had used to reach the town. The fence opening and path remained just as it had the fateful night of the events. I prepared a complaint against the railroad for allowing the fencing to become open and accessible to the students. I claimed the railroad was responsible for keeping and maintaining the fence to prevent trespassers from using the well-worn pathway from the college to the town. I also claimed that the railroad was well aware of the breach in the fence by actual notice that students had used that pathway for years. The railroad routinely inspected that stretch of rail, and as it turned out, complaints had been sent to the railroad requesting the fence be repaired. From time to time, the wall had been repeatedly repaired slipshod, only to be reopened countless times. Tragic as the boy's death was and how much it impacted his friend, it reinforced my appreciation for the dangers some youngsters don't apprehend. It's a lesson I stress to my children and grandchildren. Never mess with a train.

INSURANCE ILLUSION:

In litigation, when a person claims they were injured or damaged, they have a right to bring a lawsuit to correct the perceived wrong. Where a person has been injured or damaged under circumstances where they believe that many other people may have been hurt in the same or similar manner, they can take action for themselves or in a representative capacity for all others similarly situated. That type of litigation is known as a class action. Mostly, they are very complex and fraught with problems, which class-action defense attorneys fight with a vengeance.

Usually, the first defense is the status of the representative party. They are singled out as not representative of the entire class; they have manufactured their claim somehow, or the claim isn't subject to class-action status. The viability of the class plaintiff and the rest is also under attack from the start. Arguments about the class plaintiff's ability to represent and finance the litigation are scrutinized.

Another obstacle is that once the case is filed, the presiding judge must consider whether to certify the class.

Finance such litigation takes a significant amount of time

INSURANCE ILLUSION:

and money, and any attorney must decide whether even to attempt to file such claims.

Many years ago, we were presented with an unusual situation involving automobile insurance coverage. In Illinois, it is mandatory to purchase automobile liability insurance to obtain a license tag. The legislature passed a law that required insurers to offer customers another form of insurance entitled uninsured/underinsured motorist coverage.

Liability insurance covers the vehicle owner/driver for injuries or damages caused to others. Uninsured motorist coverage covered the owner/driver from damages or injuries caused by vehicles without liability coverage, or the coverage was denied for some reason.

Underinsured motorist coverage was fashioned to provide coverage that would protect an insured if another vehicle struck and injured or damaged the policyholder. It applied where the available coverage was insufficient to cover all their damages. An insured could purchase such coverage, at their option, up to the limit of their original liability limit.

For example, if a person purchased a liability policy for $100,000 per person / $300,000 per incident, they would have coverage over another vehicle's lesser amount of coverage. It would be typical for an insured vehicle to be covered for the minimum required limit of $25,000 per person / $50,000 per incident.

If a collision occurred between two vehicles with those coverages and an insured party had injuries worth $200,000, the at-fault driver's insurance company might pay its policy limit of $25 for any one person and the injured person with $100,000. Underinsured motorist coverage could collect an additional $75,000.00 from their policy.

Nonstandard insurers issue minimum-limit automobile liability policies. After the legislation created underinsured motorist coverage, those carriers began offering and selling underinsured motorist policies with limits of $25,000 per person/$50,000 per occurrence.

When we read the law and the policies, it became apparent that if the carrier charged a premium for such underinsured motorist coverage, they would never have to pay any benefit under those policies. The minimum liability and underinsured motorist policies would cancel each other out. Based on that theory, we filed suit as a class action against several nonstandard insurance carriers. The immediate response was unexpected and very vigorous:

They argued that their companies weren't selling that coverage but offering it at no premium.

They argued that each carrier must be sued separately.

They collectively objected to our class plaintiff, claiming that we needed a policyholder from each company we sued in order to have standing to sue them.

We were inundated with paperwork and dozens of opposing attorneys.

Discovery was no picnic either. We were sent dozens of file boxes with documents from policy pamphlets to claims reports and interoffice memoranda that nearly filled an entire office in our suite. Numerous motions were filed to disqualify us and our class plaintiff, and the issues in the case involved thousands of pages. Eventually, the case went up to the appellate court and the Supreme Court of Illinois, which condoned our theory, agreed our class plaintiff could represent at least the company that issued his policy, and sent the case back to the trial court for further disposition. After all those proceedings, the discovery of documents revealed several hundred underinsured policy purchases for premiums of a few hundred dollars, which the carrier agreed to refund. We won the battles but lost the war on the merits.

I adopted a business practice of advising my clients who were involved in motor vehicle incidents to read their policies very carefully and make sure that they had purchased not just "full coverage" but also liability insurance coverage, uninsured and underinsured coverage in a sufficient amount not less than their liability coverage, and medical payment benefits of no less than $50,000 where available.

Handicap Ramp Mishap:

Depending on age, physical condition, and other factors, a person with end-stage renal disease is usually placed on dialysis. This medical procedure is usually performed in a specialized dialysis facility. The patient must travel to the center three times a week and be placed on a machine that cleanses their blood for several hours. Many dialysis patients use wheelchairs and rely on specially equipped buses to transport them to and from the treatment centers.

I was introduced to a dialysis patient who had been hospitalized for a fractured leg. He explained that his bus had returned him to his home after dialysis, and in the unloading process, the bus operator caused him and his wheelchair to fall off the handicapped bus ramp, injuring his leg.

Special equipment is used on buses that transport disabled patients who use wheelchairs. The buses have specially designed facilities to secure the wheelchairs inside and electronic ramps, which the bus operator uses to load patients on and off the bus.

The ramp is activated by electronically opening the handicapped door at the vehicle's right rear curbside. When the bus operator reaches the patient's home, the bus operator disconnects the wheelchair and wheels it toward the side door. The door is opened, and a ramp is lowered to the floor level of the bus.

The ramp has metal flanges at both ends. When it's flush with the floor, the flange inside the bus is flat and level with the floor.

There is another metal flange on the curbside end of the ramp, which is in the up position. Then, the bus operator rolls the patient and wheelchair onto the ramp and locks the wheels.

The ramp is extended from the bus; the wheelchair is loaded onto the ramp. Once on the ramp, the bus operator lowers the patient, wheelchair, and ramp to the ground. It's crucial that when the ramp is lowered to the ground, the flange at the far end of the ramp must land on a flat surface, and then it automatically lowers to be flush with the ground to push the wheelchair off of the ramp.

The bus operator was responsible for ensuring the ramp touched the ground correctly and was flush with the ground so the wheelchair could roll off the ramp without tipping over.

In my client's case, the bus operator parked where the handicapped door was adjacent to the parkway, not on the sidewalk. When the patient, his wheelchair, and the ramp were lowered, half of the ramp touched the ground, the other half was about six inches above the ground, and the flange was not flush.

As the bus operator pushed the wheelchair and the patient off the ramp, the right wheel bumped into the upraised side of the flange, tipping the wheelchair over to the side and throwing the patient off the chair to the ground, where he fractured his leg.

The patient was taken by ambulance to a hospital and treated for the fracture and complications in his kidney disease. His mother was his court-appointed guardian, and she was referred to me by a fellow attorney.

I met with them at their house, and the history of the incident was described in detail, having been witnessed by my disabled client's mother and his caretaker, who was standing on their front porch, awaiting his arrival. I took pictures of the sidewalk and parkway area.

The fact pattern was simple. The remarkable thing that occurred was the defense arguments. First, they blamed my client's caretaker for parking his car too close to the sidewalk, so it was "impossible" to park the bus in a proper position to unload the wheelchair. The bus operator could have asked the caretaker to move his car so the bus could be parked next to the walkway. He never thought of that.

The second argument was that my client rolled himself off the ramp before it was leveled to the ground. That was interesting, if not wholly fabricated. The wheelchair had locks on the wheels, which was the bus operator's job to disengage once the wheelchair was at ground level. Additionally, the defense claimed the caretaker should have unloaded the wheelchair, which had never occurred in the five years my client was on dialysis.

The defense also claimed that the flange did lower down and that the wheelchair tipped over because of the condition of the parkway grass, which was equally implausible. The eyewitness and caretaker confirmed that one side of the flange never touched the ground. When I took the bus operator's deposition, he readily admitted to all the facts I described despite his counsel's objections to the "wrong" answers he was giving. Shortly after the deposition, negotiations commenced, and we reached an amicable resolution.

History Almost Repeats Itself:

Most attorneys read published case histories to keep current on the law. After a case has been tried if one of the parties is dissatisfied with the result of a jury verdict or an adverse ruling by a judge, they may appeal to a higher court that reviews the issues, analyzes the law, and publishes the judgments.

Those rulings may be used to support or defend a case with similar issues in the lower courts. I was particularly interested in a case involving a farm accident. The case had severe liability and discovery issues and exposed an essential aspect of litigating against big international corporations and their lawyers. It also revealed the tenacity of the injured person's attorney.

The facts of the case were straightforward. A farmer was riding on a tractor on a warm spring day. Fuel from the gas tank erupted in flames, causing severe burns. The plaintiff's attorney filed suit and engaged in extensive discovery. He requested records from the manufacturer of the tractor and previous incidents of the same type. The corporation denied it had ever received any notifications of other incidents of the same type or for any of their tractors.

They also objected because the plaintiff had yet to designate what type of tractor was involved. There are several types of farm tractors and designations, including utility tractors, harvesting tractors, planting tractors, and others, each with unique uses and characteristics. Once it was established which type of tractor was involved in the incident, the corporation again signed sworn answers that there were no previous incidents and that it had no records of such accidents.

Based on no previous accidents, the defendant moved for and received an order to dismiss the plaintiff's case.

That was devastating to the plaintiff and his attorney, but it was not the end of the story. A few years after the dismissal of the case, the same plaintiff's attorney was contacted by a farmer who had a tractor fire under almost identical conditions as the prior dismissed case.

As with the previous case, the defect was discovered on a hot spring day, and winter-grade fuel was present in the tank. The heat of the tractor and fumes from the fuel created an environment that caused the fuel to ignite.

After the new accident occurred and the suit was filed, discovery ensued. The corporate defendant again claimed it had no incident reports or prior accidents of unexplained, spontaneous tractor fires.

The plaintiff's attorney was astonished. He had personal knowledge of his prior case, went before the presiding judge with the denials, and presented the documents from his earlier case. The judge ordered the corporate executives who had signed the previous denials to appear for their sworn statements, at which point the corporate officers exposed the truth behind their denials.

All incident reports, previous complaints, and documentation about other accidents were sent to the corporation's attorneys for storage so the corporate officers could truthfully swear they did not possess the documentation.

HISTORY ALMOST REPEATS ITSELF:

The attorney was given access to the attorney's offices and found dozens of boxes of files with records of similar incidents and similar claims, including the previously dismissed case. With those discoveries, the plaintiff's attorney obtained an order compelling the corporation and its attorneys to turn over the original case file from the prior dismissed action and immediately reinstated that claim. In addition, they were ordered to produce copies of the documents from similar tractor fires, which led to significant settlements for the previously injured farmer and the new plaintiff.

I continually remind myself of that case and those decisions whenever I pursue discovery against corporate defendants. I adopted a policy to always inquire about document storage and arrangements, retention policies, and the identity of all employees who actively participate in the periodic destruction of documents.

Memorable Clients

TESTIFYING WHILE INTOXICATED

In another car crash case that I filed, I represented a gentleman who, I sensed, tended to have one or two after a hard day's work, so I was cautious to prepare him about how the case would proceed. We met in my office several times to prepare his testimony. Throughout those preparation sessions, I stressed that the trial would last at least the whole day and the various steps in the proceedings.

I stressed that a jury trial would be unfamiliar to him, and he might be nervous speaking in front of a jury, but our preparation sessions would help acquaint him so he'd be comfortable. I explained each step—the jury selection, how each side would have an opportunity to question potential jurors and the opening statement both attorneys would give. Once the jury had been selected, he would be seated in the witness chair next to the judge, and I would start asking him questions for which he was prepared. We practiced the questions numerous times, including his answers, the documents I would show him during his testimony, and how he would describe the photographs of his vehicle and the other vehicle. I told him to be attentive during the jury selection process and to the potential jurors. After each jury panel member was questioned, I would consult with him, and we would decide which jurors to choose and which to eliminate. He would become more relaxed once the process began and shouldn't be uncomfortable. All he had to do was concentrate, pay attention, and do his best.

After the jurors were selected and sworn in, I gave my opening statement, and the defense counsel did likewise. Then, it was time for my client to testify. To my surprise, his testimony was clear and understandable. The trial testimony began around 10:30 a.m. I stood at the far end of the jury box, so my client would have to speak up and project to allow me and all jurors to hear him. My questions were asked in short, clear sentences, and he responded as well as any witness I had ever questioned. He was conversational and made eye contact with the jurors, and we went through his testimony with almost flawless precision. He did very well, and the jury heard my client's best version on his behalf.

The judge, sensing the approach of the noon lunch hour, asked my opponent and me if it would be an appropriate time after my questioning ended to take a break and begin the cross-examination after lunch. We all agreed, and the judge discharged the jury until 2:00 p.m. when the trial would reconvene. As usual, the judge gave the standard admonition to the jury not to discuss the case or the testimony they'd heard thus far with anyone, including each other, a standard warning.

My client was hungry, and I hardly ever ate anything during a trial, so I directed him to several local restaurants and told him to meet me around 1:30 p.m. at my office, a block away from the courthouse. We'd review a few points I anticipated the defense counsel would ask him. Around 1:30 p.m., my client appeared at my office as instructed. However, he was intoxicated. His eyes were bloodshot, his speech was slurred, and he was a little disoriented and shaky, but his appearance's most apparent element was his stink. He reeked from a considerable distance. When he entered our offices, my secretary sprayed air fresheners in the entire suite.

Panic is one word to describe my horror, and fear is another. How could I get him to the courthouse and submit him for cross-examination? I didn't know what to do. We started back to the courthouse and passed a local drugstore. I went into the store and bought cans of Lysol, air freshener, and deodorant and got back to the courtroom as quickly as I could with my client in tow. When we reached the courtroom, I walked him up to the witness box to avoid him walking past the soon-to-be seated jurors.

When the court reconvened, I stepped up to the bench and asked to reopen my proofs so my client could testify to additional facts about his job.

I asked my client, "What are your job duties?" In his slurred, halting way, the spoke of his cleaning activities and what materials he used, like mops and brooms, air sprays, and deodorants. I took out the cans of aerosols I had just purchased and some paper towels and began spraying the towels with the substances to cover the room with flowery scents and sprays. Then, I passed the soaked towels among the jurors to cover the stench of his present state.

I wouldn't have been able to cover up the glassy red eyes, the slurred speech, his bright, red nose, or his slovenly appearance, so I asked a few more simple questions and rested our case.

I felt physical pain when the defense counsel began his questioning of my client. It could have been an episode of a sitcom. My client needed help understanding or being able to respond to the most straightforward questions. He yawned openly. His nose was bright red, and he needed a nap. He looked like a deer in the headlights the whole time, trying to focus on the defendant's attorney, who kept walking around the well of the courtroom, causing my client to try to follow his movements. It was laughable and pitiful at the same time.

After about fifteen minutes of this production, the defendant rested, and my client was excused to return to the desk where I was seated. Fearful that he might fall over walking back, I assisted him, and we sat down.

It only took the jury a short time to decide against us. But to this day, whenever I meet the defendant's attorney in court, on the street, or at social gatherings, he reminds me of the event in good humor. Even so, the scars remain.

Executive Decisions

In the plaintiff's personal injury litigation, the oddest and often unexpected events arise from unexpected sources. Our practice received the usual car crash cases, calls from people who fall and get hurt, and inquiries about other incidents.

So, it was unusual for me to have the firm's senior partner give me the telephone number of one of his wealthy friends who had an accident at his home, which my boss wanted me to investigate. The only information I had was the man's name and telephone number, and the incident involved a defect in a product, a subject with which I was familiar.

The gentleman was in the hospital with severe injuries to his hands, and I needed to get all the facts. If we could pursue a lawsuit, I should go to the hospital to sign up for the injury case. I knew this man had built an enormous Internet company, which was now a public company, and he owned a massive mansion on the lake, owned a private jet, and drove the most expensive cars.

I called the number, and the man who answered seemed groggy and spoke slowly. He said he was taking heavy pain medication and needed some rest, which explained his speech

Leo Bleiman

difficulty. He told me that he had injured both hands and wanted to sue the manufacturer of his gas-powered lawn mower. I asked him the make and model and told him I'd do some quick research on the Internet, focusing on the user's manual and the warranties that came with the machine, and told him I'd call him back. We've all seen the type of lawn mower with a motor on top of a platform; underneath is a rotating blade that cuts the grass and discharges the cut grass through a side opening into a bag or cage to catch the clippings. At that point, I didn't know how the injuries occurred other than it involved both hands.

After I familiarized myself with the lawn mower's operating characteristics and details, I called him back to find out more about how the accident happened.

To present a claim for a product defect, a person must show that the product had a defect when it left the manufacturer's control. There are numerous defenses to product defect claims, one of which is product misuse. There is also a theory of improper warnings on a product.

When I called the potential client, he was much more articulate and related his complaints about the mower.

He was home with nothing better to do and noticed his lawn looked overgrown as his gardener hadn't mowed it. It was a bright, clear spring day without a cloud in the sky, so he decided to mow the lawn himself. He entered his garage, filled the lawn mower with gas, and cut the grass. He'd almost finished; the grass looked fine, but the hedges along the driveway were overgrown and uneven. Figuring that the mower would be the perfect tool to trim the hedges, he bent down to pick the mower while it was still running and placed his hands around the blade cover, whereupon the blade lacerated the ends of the fingers on each of his hands.

To make the ridiculous situation even more ludicrous, he had sent me photographs of the mower, which had emblazoned on top of the blade cover, in three different places, in giant bright red letters, "WARNING: DO NOT PLACE FINGERS OR HANDS ON OR NEAR THE BLADES."

Sometimes, even the brightest of our brethren do the dumbest things. This one topped the list.

Testifying in Style

It took several experiences to learn that you should tend your own garden and leave other gardeners to grow theirs. It was always a humbling experience to undertake cases in counties outside my local jurisdiction. It didn't matter how near or far they were; local judges favored local lawyers. So, as a young attorney, from time to time, I made errors in judgment when handling a case in a different county. Usually, if a case occurs elsewhere, the best tactic is to locate a local attorney in that jurisdiction and have them handle it since they're familiar with the population, the judges, and the local court rules.

I represented four African-American ladies who had been in a crash with a truck as they approached a road construction site in far southern Illinois. My clients were slightly ahead of a tanker truck on the interstate highway, heading back to Chicago from a trip to Arkansas. The tanker truck hit their vehicle from behind as they approached a construction with barriers blocking their lane. All four were injured, taken to a local hospital, treated for a few days, and then released. My clients were from my county, and the truck driver was driving over the road from a different state. He was also injured and treated in the same local hospital as my clients.

By the time the clients, driver, and all the passengers retained me, the truck driver had filed a lawsuit in the county where the crash happened. It was in the southernmost county in Illinois. So, my case had to be filed in the same county, and the cases were consolidated for trial. The driver of my client's vehicle had insurance to cover the truck driver's claims. Her insurance company retained a grizzled, senior attorney to defend her from the truck driver's suit. I represented them for their injury claims. The tanker truck company hired an attorney to protect my client's claims, and the driver hired a local attorney to recover damages for his injuries.

All three lawyers for the defense and the truck driver's attorney were local, and all were friends. I was the interloper. We went through the discovery process relatively quickly, and the case was set for a jury trial. I drove almost three hundred miles to the county courthouse the day before the trial began. I met with my client's defense counsel in his office across the street from the courthouse. We also met with the opposing attorneys over dinner, which was a nice gesture. We had a cordial conversation and agreed to meet at the courthouse the following day at ten to review the witnesses' scheduling, and they called the judge to tell him what we planned to do.

About a week before the trip downstate, I met with the clients in my office to prepare them for their testimony. We spent almost an entire day reviewing the facts of the collision and how the vehicles came together. They told me about the road construction, the details of the crash, how their car and the tanker truck both rolled over on the side of the road, and how the chemicals from the car sprayed all over them, causing them to not only their physical injuries and red, swollen rashes they claimed from being sprayed with chemicals that had spilled out of the truck.

I made it a point to mention to my clients that we were

going downstate to a rural courthouse in a very conservative county. The jury would mainly consist of residents and farmers, and there probably would be few African Americans in the pool. Even if there were, the defense attorneys would use challenges to exclude them from the trial.

I also told them they should wear appropriate clothes for the trial—no jeans or sweatshirts but dresses like those they would wear to a business meeting or church. They left my office, and we agreed to meet at their defense attorney's office the morning of the trial so he could meet them and go over some trial matters, like scheduling their testimony. We decided to have the driver testify first and then the passengers.

On the day of the trial, I went to the office of my client's defense attorney to discuss the impending trial. We were sitting in his office when his secretary came in with a dazed expression, which I could only describe as white with shock.

She said, "I hate interrupting your conference, but your clients are here." "That's fine,' said the defense attorney. "We'll be out there in a few minutes and then leave for court."

"Well," the secretary continued, "I think you ought to come out to the lobby and meet them to discuss things before that."

"No, that's okay," said the lawyer. "We'll finish up in here."

The exasperated secretary said, "I think you should come out now." "Oh, all right," he said. We both reluctantly stood up and headed for his office waiting room.

When we entered his reception area, I almost fainted. My knees started shaking, and I couldn't formulate any words. There they were, all four of our clients, seated on a bench, each dressed in identical bright orange gospel singing robes that flowed to the ground, with starched white collars. With the most composure I have ever seen, the defense lawyer greeted the clients and said, "Good morning, ladies. It's so nice to see you all here bright and early, and I must say, those are mighty nice dresses you all have."

"Thank you, sir," they all said.

"You know," the lawyer continued, since I was speechless, "in a few minutes, we're going over to the courthouse, and we're going to have a jury trial. The jurors will want to hear your testimony, and we want to ensure they aren't confused as to whether you're there to testify or sing. So, it'd be best if you had something different to wear. We can ask the judge to hold off a little while so you could go back and change into something different for the trial." When I regained my ability to speak, I told the lawyer what I had said to the clients at our preparation session, and he calmed me down.

The trial lasted four days, and we ultimately lost, but the event was an experience for a lifetime. In the postmortem, after the verdict was announced, the defense lawyer told me I had done a superb job wrenching the testimony out of my clients' mouths and not to feel bad, but it still stung.

Beyond a Reasonable Doubt

As a young attorney, I handled many cases in other disciplines before concentrating on personal and work injury cases. I occasionally dealt with divorce cases, eviction matters, real estate closings, and very few criminal cases.

I never handled a traffic case to defend an intoxicated driver. However, I've had personal injury cases against drunk drivers. I thought drunken drivers were usually the least injured in car crashes. It was against my principles to use my knowledge and skill as an attorney to put a driver back on the streets and highways, knowing alcohol intoxication is a hard habit to break. Once drunk drivers are absolved of the charge, they will likely get drunk and drive again. I didn't want that on my conscience.

A former client of mine contacted me to represent her in an alleged shoplifting case. She was an African-American woman charged with retail theft. My client visited a women's clothing store in Melrose Park, Illinois. Melrose Park is a predominantly white community with a solid Italian demographic. It's a very tight-knit enclave located west of Chicago.

My client visited a women's clothing store to shop. She was looking for a knitted sweater and was interested in some displayed on hangers on circular racks throughout the store. The price tags were attached to each shirt with a plastic thread woven through the fabric in a loop through the sleeve. After walking around the store, my client located a sweater she liked and brought it to the cashier to pay for it. The sale was completed, and my client started to leave the store. As she left the store, a white security guard/loss prevention employee stopped her and asked what was in my client's bag.

My client removed the sweater with the attached price tag and a receipt for the purchase price. In a loud and belligerent voice, the security guard said, "You're under arrest for changing the sweater's price from its original price to a lower price. I've called the police. Come with me." She escorted my client into the store manager's office and waited. The police arrived, took her to the local police station, and booked her for retail theft, and she posted a bond. A court hearing date was assigned.

While sitting in the manager's office, my client tried to recreate the crime they claimed she had committed. The guard explained that she was watching my client as she was shopping, and when my client approached the sweaters on the rack, the guard claimed she was watching my client the entire time. She said she saw my client furtively look around the store back and forth, never looking at the price tag, and in the process, the guard claimed my client unraveled the price tag from the sweater and replaced it with a lower price.

It was the ultimate understatement to say she was shocked and humiliated by the accusation. The police handcuffed her, removed her from the store in front of the other customers, and took her to the police station. She sat at the police station in a cell until her husband came to post a bond and allowed her to be released. The next day, she called my office, and we set an appointment to meet and discuss the case. I had known this woman for years, and from my dealings with her, I knew she was not the type of person who would do that crime. She and her husband were each employed, they owned their own home, and she lived an exemplary life.

When we sat down to discuss the charges, my client's shame and humiliation still haunted her. I reviewed the criminal complaint, which indicated it was theft under a certain amount and was a misdemeanor. Still, I informed her that a misdemeanor of stealing was a crime of dishonesty, which, if she were convicted, would follow her in her life, her job, and whatever the future held for her. She was even more upset when I informed her of the consequences, but I had an obligation to be forthright in explaining the gravity of the charges placed against her.

The case came up for preliminary matters and to set a trial date. The hearing was in a courtroom in Melrose Park, and I learned the presiding judge was a resident of that town. All the other court personnel, including the court reporter, were white. When a criminal charge is brought, the prosecution must disclose the witnesses they intend to call and produce documents or materials they plan to offer into evidence.

I knew the prosecution would call the security guard, and they had the garment with the price tag attached to it, which formed the basis of the theft charges.

I looked over the sweater very carefully. The shirt had the price tag with the allegedly altered price tag. It was made from a knitted fabric, and the price tag was affixed by a plastic thread threaded through the knitted fabric. I concluded from my inspection of the price tag, and the plastic loop that is removing it would have been impossible without breaking the plastic thread or tearing the tag.

The prosecutor approached me and offered a plea arrangement. She offered to reduce the charges if my client would sign an admission to the crime (which would be on her record as a conviction) and promised never to enter that store again.

I presented that proposal to my client. After discussing the risks and benefits of entering into that agreement, she declined and authorized me to reject the plea agreement offer and proceed with the trial.

About a month later, we appeared at the same courthouse and courtroom with the judge who had heard the preliminary matters, and the trial commenced. It was a bench trial, not before a jury. Those proceedings command the judge to be both the trier of fact and the official judging the law applicable to the case. I couldn't avoid scanning the onlookers in the courtroom, who were all local, white townspeople.

The prosecutor called her first witness, the white woman security guard. She took the witness stand, was sworn in, and began testifying in response to the prosecutor's questions. Her testimony was scripted.

She gave the details of what she claimed occurred. She said she watched my client approach the round rack in the middle of the store, and my client was standing next to the sweaters on the display carousel. My client's eyes darted around the store, never looking down at the sweater. This went on for about a minute. Then my client raised the sweater to her eye level, looked it over once or twice, turned it backward and forward, examined it, and then carried it to the cashier. The security guard watched the cashier ring up the price on the tag, and my client paid. The cashier put the sweater into a bag and handed it to my client, who proceeded toward the exit door. Then, the guard stopped my client and accused her of the theft.

The prosecutor asked supporting questions about the guard's training, job duties, and responsibilities. She then went through the details of the guard's actions, completing an incident report and verifying that everything on it was true and accurate. The prosecutor closed her questioning, and it was my turn to cross-examine the guard.

I stood up and requested permission from the judge to approach the witness, which he granted. I started my questioning by asking the guard if, when my client was standing next to the sweater display, my client ever looked downward. The guard said no. I wondered if the plastic thread had been broken. The guard answered no. I asked if the price tag my client was accused of changing had been torn. The guard said no. I wondered how long the incident took, and she said, "Less than a minute." I then asked the guard to verify whether the sweater that was introduced into evidence was the exact sweater that had the alleged adulterated lower price tag on it. She identified it accordingly. She confirmed that the price on the tag was lower than the other sweaters from that same rack and that the price tag and plastic thread were in pristine condition—no cuts, no breaks, and no tears whatsoever.

"Now then, Officer, using whatever means available to you, taking as much time as you like, and looking as intently as you can at the sweater and price tag in front of you, please remove the price tag on that sweater without breaking the plastic thread or tearing the price tag."

Then, I walked back to my seat at the counsel table. I wanted to allow her as much time as she liked to try to accomplish that task. She reluctantly took the sweater from me and proceeded to remove the tag. She twisted the sweater in several directions, turned it around, pushed the tag, pushed the plastic thread, put the garment upside down in her lap, and tried every technique to remove the price tag or the plastic thread for the next ten minutes. I just sat there, looking at her growing frustration and the judge watching this demonstration, like everyone else in the courtroom. Finally, in frustration, the guard ripped the tag off the sweater. I said, "No more questions, Your Honor. Let the record show the guard has torn the price tag off the sweater."

"Duly noted, Counsel," said the judge.

At the end of a trial, each side presents closing arguments to the judge sitting at a bench trial. The closing argument is the attorney's last opportunity to comment on the evidence in the case and suggest how to construe that evidence. Each side emphasizes how the evidence supports the client's position. The prosecution went first and focused on the employment and professionalism of the guard; her observations and their proof proved, beyond a reasonable doubt, that my client was guilty.

In a criminal case, the prosecution has the burden of proof to prove that the offense has been proven beyond any reasonable doubt as to each element of the crime, in this case, retail theft. The prosecutor glossed over the demonstration when the guard couldn't remove the price tag without tearing it.

When I started my closing argument, I stressed that the proofs established overwhelming doubt that the crime was accomplished as the guard had described it. My client had not been looking down at the sweater when the alleged change in the price tag occurred. Even when the guard had all the time in the world, looking at the tag and the plastic thread, she couldn't change the price without tearing one or the other. It obviously couldn't have been done in less than one minute while not looking intently at the tag and the plastic thread. The guard had said the sweater's price was less than others on the same rack. That fact had relevance to the charge only if every other sweater had been admitted in evidence. No factual basis existed for this charge, and my client should be found "not guilty." I thanked the judge for the opportunity to present the case, and I sat down. My client was delighted with my argument, and it was time for the judge to render his judgment.

The judge began, "I watched this case develop very carefully. I was particularly impressed with the demonstration presented by the defense. So, I conclude that significant doubt exists about the charges brought here. But I have to consider whether my doubt is reasonable doubt."

I asked myself, "WHAT?"

"So," he continued, "I believe she's guilty. Finding for the prosecution." I almost fell off my chair.

My client and I stumbled out of the courtroom, astonished at what had happened. I told my client she had a right to appeal, and she should. Once a judge comments that he doubts guilt or innocence, the decision should be for the defendant.

Eventually, she accepted her fate and didn't appeal, which was a bitter pill. When I contemplated the case, even months after the trial, I could only conclude the cards were stacked against her the minute she walked into the store in that community. It was an eye-opening experience of life in the big city. Years later the trial still bothered me. At some point, I realized it could have simply been a cheaper sweater that was hung on the wrong rack. You live and learn.

Patty Melt from Hell

A young nursing student's family contacted me about their daughter being hospitalized in Peoria, Illinois. My previous experiences taught me not to engage in cases far outside my local county. However, I had previously represented the family, and they begged me to speak with her. I drove to Peoria to meet with her and her parents in the hospital. The girl was a victim of food poisoning, but she could only relate to her parents or me where she had eaten. She was paralyzed from the neck down, could hardly speak, and lost her ability to stand or walk. Her central nervous system had completely shut down. The girl had eaten at a food court in a shopping mall and, within a few hours, had developed a severe debilitating condition from a bacterial infection later identified as botulism.

Her medical bills were already over $100,000, and she had no group health insurance. Her health situation was dire. She faced months of intensive care and rehabilitation if she could respond to treatment. I started to investigate the possible causes of her infection and consulted with local lawyers who had clients in similar illness states, all from the same type of incident. A few of the patrons had already died.

We collected resources, including the health department, local authorities, and the CDC. In these cases, samples are sent to the CDC for evaluation and testing. Their findings are usually admissible and persuasive. The samples confirmed the cause of the infection. Botulism needs some vacuum to grow, and no potential sources were readily apparent. The local health department did extensive testing, and no botulinum toxin was found at first. Only one potential source remained after testing the entire restaurant kitchen, which was submitted for testing and returned positive.

All the patrons who got sick had eaten "patty melt" sandwiches. A patty melt sandwich is a hamburger with cheese and grilled onions, then placed on rye bread and toasted on a flat-top grill. The restaurant owner had a habit of grilling onions and putting the newly grilled onions on top of previously cooked onions left on the grill at the end of a previous day (or days). The batch of onions was then reheated and placed on the sandwiches. In this case, the pressure of the layers of onions was sufficient to form a vacuum where the bacteria grew, polluting the onions with the organism.

The case bears mentioning here because there was a very serious legal question about the insurance coverage for the circumstances—the number of cases numbered in the dozens. Three people had died, and there were dozens of injuries, like my clients. The issue involved the interpretation of the insurance policy. The restaurant had a $1 million liability policy and a $ 500,000 excess umbrella policy.

The attorneys for the insurance carrier argued that the $1.5 million in coverage applied to all the cases together. We argued that each sandwich was a separate incident and that each claim benefited from protection up to $1.5 million, which would have exposed the insurer to tens of millions of dollars in risk. The trial court agreed with the plaintiffs that each sandwich was a separate claim and affirmed on appeal, giving each plaintiff the right to claim the total limit of the liability policy and excess umbrella coverage. As soon as the appellate court issued the decision, the insurer aggressively contacted each plaintiff's counsel and negotiated settlements.

It was disclosed during our negotiations to resolve my client's claim that the premium paid for the insurance policies was less than $500. The restaurant never reopened. My client eventually recovered through extensive physical and occupational therapy, and she completed her nursing education and became a registered nurse, saving lives.

The Cesspool

Most municipal park districts have limited budgets. A client told me about her son's serious injury in a park district swimming pool. His visit was near the end of the swimming season. He dove into the pool's deep end during the swim session and struck his head on the bottom. He was underwater for several minutes before lifeguards noticed him. When they retrieved him, he was given CPR, revived, and taken to a local hospital for tests.

During his hospital stay, he received extensive testing and cognitive examinations. His IQ was measured at 60. His mother said he was physically and mentally fine before the incident, but since then, he had been "slow." He needed considerable assistance in school and countless hours of rehabilitation. We filed suit against the park district that ran the pool and started our investigation. Reports from the paramedics indicated that the pool water was cloudy and murky when he dove in, which led me to visit the storage facility of the park district and review all the maintenance records for the pool. I scoured numerous boxes of documents and discovered that the budget allowed maintenance on the pool filter and pump at the start of the swim season, and the filter needed repair that had yet to be performed.

Consequently, the negligent maintenance of the pool equipment was the cause of the cloudy, murky condition, which prevented my client's son from seeing the bottom and avoiding injury. We claimed in our lawsuit that the child had suffered a brain injury, and the proof was in the IQ testing. During the suit's discovery phase, I prepared and sent a subpoena to the board of education, which my client's son attended. Still, they claimed that the law prevented me or anyone else from obtaining the records.

With no countervailing evidence to present as a defense, the opposing counsel and I negotiated a settlement, which provided significant damages for my client's unique needs. A judge approved the case for settlement, and the money was placed into an account in the minor's name, with the provision that any withdrawals had to be approved by the court.

My client's mother was thrilled, and I was gratified to have prevailed. Usually, that would be the end of the story. However, almost a year after resolving the case, I received a certified mail package from the Board of Education containing my minor client's school records.

I was bewildered as to why they had complied with my subpoena in the first place and curious as to what those records showed. The records showed that my minor client was given special assistance before the near drowning. To my utter amazement, he had been tested for his intelligence several times—his listed IQ results from before the near drowning was 50.

I sent the confidential records to the mother so that she could keep the papers, for her own use.

And Four of Those

My first office was in an office building that did not have automatic elevators. The building had manual elevator operators. The elevator car didn't even have a door on it. As you rode up and down, you could see the door on each floor as you passed during your trip. My office was on the top floor of the building.

The gentlemen who operated the elevators were always cordial and polite. They ranged in age from retirees working to keep busy, to college students earning money until they graduated. Others were sad sacks who had reached the level of their competence. One late afternoon, as I was reviewing files for court for the next day, one of the young men appeared in my office after his shift ended. He asked me if I had time to discuss a legal problem; he thought I could assist.

When he came into my office, he was still wearing his building's standard uniform and sat down to tell me his situation. He thanked me for meeting with him and then explained that he had been arrested by the police a few days earlier at the building.

He told me he had gone into the men's bathroom for a comfort break, and while urinating, one of the female custodians had entered the bathroom unannounced. She saw him standing there, screamed at him, and called the police, claiming that Bill (not his real name) had exposed himself to her. "A total fabrication," according to Bill.

He handed me the complaint against him, charging him with "indecent exposure," which provided me with the statement and details from my client's version and the custodian's. The notice identified the court and the court date. I explained to Bill that I didn't actively practice criminal defense law, but if it were merely a misunderstanding, perhaps I could be of assistance to him. I explained, if it was too involved, I would recommend a colleague of mine who concentrated his practice on criminal defense work.

I must mention that Bill's version of the incident differed widely from that of the female custodians. She claimed she was in the general locker room when Bill appeared with his unfettered manhood hanging in the breeze, and he approached her, which caused her to scream and call the management office, who called the police, and the arrest ensued. Who to believe?

I felt I needed some historical information to get a complete picture of Bill's background. I asked him if he had previous encounters with the police or any other charges or convictions against him. He was very forthright in telling me that he was a rambunctious youth and occasionally had "station adjustments" for disorderly conduct a few times before he took an interest in school. He was enrolled in a community college, working as an elevator operator in our building to pay his tuition. I had no reason to doubt that information. However, thinking back over the conversation, Bill was almost thirty at the time, so truth be told, I might have been a little naive.

More to the point, he described his activities during the entire day before the alleged washroom incident in detail, every step of his routine, from his arrival and punching the time clock to his lunch break up to the alleged exposure.

I also asked if there were any other things, he needed to tell me about his criminal history that I should know about if I were to undertake his representation.

He said, "No, not, except for four more of those," pointing to the complaint for "indecent exposure" he had handed me at the start of our conversation.

I said, "You've had four other indecent exposure charges?" He said, "No, convictions."

"Bill," I said, "I think you'll need the name of my colleague." so I gave him the name of my friend who only practiced criminal defense and sent Bill on his way.

Auntie Misbehavin'

My aunt was in her late eighties when she called me one day at work. She was about four feet tall and frail. I had only been practicing for a few years, making little money and handling many cases. I did real estate closings, collection cases, forcible entry, detainer-rent collection cases, traffic court matters, and personal injury cases. It was unusual for Auntie to call me at work. I didn't think she even knew my phone number. When I picked up the phone, I could hear turmoil in her voice.

"Can you help me out?" she asked.

"I'll try if I can," I said. "What is the problem?" "I'm in jail," she said.

I almost fell out of my chair. Astonished, I asked, "What for?"

She explained, she had gone to a large, well-known department store in the downtown area, to purchase a tablecloth and napkins. She had picked up the tablecloth, went to another counter to pick out the napkins, and mistakenly or inadvertently placed the tablecloth into her bag. When she didn't find the napkins to match, she left the store, which was when the store loss prevention personnel "nabbed" her. The guards handcuffed her, placed her in a holding cell in the store, and called the police department to take her to the police station. I could only imagine the scene.

Luckily, I had enough money in my checking account to cash a check and go to the police station to bail her out. When she was brought out of the holding cell at the police station by an officer around six feet, three inches tall, she looked shaken, embarrassed, and minuscule. Before I had a chance to speak, she shook her finger at me and swore me to secrecy, not to divulge the details of this incident to anyone in our family.

I drove her home, and she repeated her admonition. Then she gave me a copy of the complaint against her: "Shoplifting." We had a court date about a month later.

On the court date, I approached the prosecutor, explained that the defendant was my aunt, and suggested this was merely an oversight of an eighty-plus-year-old heavily medicated woman. I argued that my aunt hadn't taken the tablecloth intentionally and that this was simply negligence on her part and didn't warrant the aggressive actions of the store. The prosecuting attorney was very understanding, but her hands were tied since the complaining witness was the store loss prevention officer. The store's policy was to fully prosecute every case, no matter how small the amount or age of the culprit.

When our case was called, we approached the bench. I introduced myself and my aunt to the judge. The judge read the complaint and asked me if my client was present in court, even though she was standing beside me. I said, "This is my aunt, Your Honor." I gave him her name.

The judge stood up from his chair and craned his neck to the front of his desk to see her. When he did, he turned to the prosecutor and said, "Do we have a problem here?" After that, the prosecutor explained that the store insisted on prosecuting every case.

The judge turned to the store employee and the

Auntie Misbehavin'

prosecutor and said, "I know stores like yours have a policy, but considering the circumstances here, at her age, I don't think this lady is embarking on a criminal lifestyle, and I'm going to order her to not shop in that store anymore. This case is dismissed."

Although the store employee wasn't happy, I was thrilled, and so was my aunt. Case closed. Years later, my aunt died. I never mentioned this incident to my wife or any of our family. After the funeral, when we all had paid our respects, and the memorial concluded, I related the incident to my wife, cousins, and children at the memorial dinner. After the initial shock, we all howled in laughter. From then on, we fondly referred to her as the Jailbird.

Morning Joe

From the ridiculous to the sublime, all cases are a mystery. Some cases settle before a lawsuit is filed, and some take years to resolve, favorably or unfavorably.

A client came to our office with a very unusual story. The circumstances were quite simple. Like every other morning, he went to his local convenience store near his house for his morning cup of coffee and a sweet roll. The store had a self-service coffee bar. The counter had a coffee maker and individual pitchers on separate burners to keep the coffee hot. The pitchers were standard glass bowls with a hand grip for the customers to pick up their selection and pour their serving. There were different pitchers with various coffee flavors: Columbian, hazelnut, decaffeinated, and French vanilla. There were even pitchers of hot water for tea drinkers. There were multiple sweeteners, creamers, stirrers, napkins, and a buffet for the discerning coffee drinker. My client said he visited the store daily and was intimately familiar with the self-serve process.

On the day of his incident, he claimed he went to the store, picked up his medium-sized insulated coffee cup, and placed his hand on the handle of the hazelnut coffee pot. As he described it, he had the hot, steaming pot of coffee full to the brim. As he lifted the coffeepot to pour into the cup in his hand, the bowl separated from the handle and poured the entire pot of steaming hot coffee onto his body, from his waist down his pants, scalding his legs and his private parts. He screamed in pain, and the clerk came over with a broom and mop to clean up the glass and mop up the spilled coffee from the floor.

My client raced out of the store and went home in agony as the hot coffee was still on his clothes and soaking through his pants and underwear. He visited an emergency room, which provided immediate care and gave him salves and ointments to place on the burns, and he was sent home to heal. He called to work, told his boss of his unfortunate event, and stayed home.

A few days later, he contacted me and told me about his incident and his injuries. We exchanged some documents to represent him, and we sent a notice to the store and its insurance carrier. Within a few days, I received a telephone call from an adjuster at the insurance claim office, and we exchanged some critical information about the claim. When I informed the adjuster of the nature of the injuries, he was immediately dismissive and didn't accept our theory or that the accident even occurred. He added that if my client suffered any injury, as he had claimed, the adjuster would need photographs of the injuries.

I telephoned my client and informed him that the adjuster wanted more proof of the incident and the injuries. Without hesitation, my client described the entire layout of the store: the position of the cashier, the merchandise displays, the location of the coffee station, the beer coolers, and the frozen food freezers. He also named the maker of the coffee pot he had been using. He swore he was absolutely confident about the coffee maker.

Then, I informed my client that the adjuster wanted to see

pictures of the scalding injuries. I asked him to take a few, very discreet—I emphasized discreet—colored photographs to show images of the location and severity of the injuries. I asked him to send me those pictures if there were still blisters or scars. He said he'd try to get some. After my conversation, I attended to other matters and forgot about the case. The next episode in the coffee pot saga occurred about three weeks later.

At the time of my client's incident, I had three twenty-ish female secretaries and staff assistants. All I remember was the time. It was about one in the afternoon, and the mail had just been delivered to our office. Usually, the secretary at the front desk would receive and open the mail and then distribute it to me and the others in the office. I heard some laughter, then nothing. After a few seconds, there was more laughter. After a few of those outbursts, there were several loud howls of laughter, and all three of my female staff were standing at the front desk in uncontrollable hilarity, their laughter booming throughout the office. Every second, a new roar would emerge.

I couldn't imagine what had occurred. As I exited my office and walked up to the front desk, my secretary handed me the cause of their reactions.

She handed me an envelope that contained no less than thirty-six five-by-seven colored whole-body photographs of my client standing stark naked, exposing his genitals in stark reality, holding his maleness with a pen, consisting of images from the front, back, sides, under, over, and all around the swollen red member.

I stood there in complete shock, sheepishly taking the envelope and placing it in his file, which I hoped would never be displayed again.

Thankfully, the photographs never saw the light of day. I returned them to the client in a hermetically sealed envelope, with warnings all over the package marked Confidential. The saving grace for me occurred a few weeks later. My client had provided me with the name of the coffee maker and the coffee pot, which he swore, under oath, was the culprit that caused his injury. The insurance carrier produced documentation from the store, which proved that they only had one type of coffee maker and coffee pot, and it was a completely different manufacturer than the one my client claimed injured him. Case dropped and dismissed, thankfully.

Unintended Consequences

Sometimes, the best intentions turn out to be far worse than expected. A substantial corporate enterprise decided to improve a housing development in a municipality where gang violence was rampant. It wasn't wholly altruistic since the tenant population was primarily underprivileged, and the government paid their rent. The improvement and redevelopment of the property was a small investment in the rental income the corporate giant would get in return. This was intended to be a win-win situation. The property lay between two rival gang areas and was disputed turf. Shootings, stabbings, thefts, and assaults occurred frequently, and police knew this was one of the worst areas to patrol or enforce the law.

My client was a young man with obvious learning disabilities. He was living with his mother, hadn't finished high school, had no job, and spent most of his days playing basketball and video games, although he was well past the age of majority. He was not in one of the rival gangs competing for the turf where he lived. Unfortunately, being of his generation and living in that area, if a gang member was in the area and spotted a male who was not a member of his gang, it was assumed that he was in the rival gang and, thus, a target.

One afternoon, my client was walking from a convenience store to his apartment when he was spotted by a gang enforcer who calmly walked up behind him and shot him in the neck, rendering my client a quadriplegiac. The mother came to me to see if there was a viable case against the gang member or the gang. The shooter was identified as a known gangster and arrested. The arrest was memorable in that a few months after my client's incident, the shooter engaged the police in an open gunfight in the housing development where the events had transpired. Of course, the shooter had no assets and was uncollectible, even if we sued him.

We researched the events surrounding the corporate entity undertaking the renovation and redevelopment efforts. We found some interesting facts that supported a theory of recovery against the developer. They had removed the single-armed entry guard station and the perimeter safety fencing surrounding the housing units. They had removed the closed-circuit security system. They established an incident reporting system to document every violent incident involving a tenant or intruder on the property. Armed with that documentation and photographic evidence, we filed suit.

After all the various parties appeared and answered our complaint, discovery was ensured. We issued subpoenas for all police records and daily security service reports and requested the depositions of management personnel and supervisors at the property.

When significant discovery occurs in a extreme injury cases, it is customary for the parties to meet and confer to organize the discovery into phases and manage the litigation in some sequence and order. In this case, we anticipated at least fifty or more witnesses had to be deposed, including investigating police officers, gang unit officials, countless physicians, therapists, psychologists, pain management personnel, and other specialists we'd have to depose.

We suggested such a meeting once the written discovery concluded in our case, and the defendants' counsel agreed to a in person meeting to establish such a schedule. In my invitation to the meet-and-confer session, I ended my letter with a statement I often include: We are always open to good faith, reasonable, and fruitful discussions about resolving the case amicably at any time in the litigation.

The meeting was more cordial than I expected. We laid out a plan, identifying the names of the people we intended to depose and the dates for their depositions. We set a timetable, which projected at least a two-year schedule to complete the preliminary work and prepare the case for an eventual jury trial. We stood to leave, thanked the attorneys for their anticipated cooperation, and departed.

One of our opponents stopped us as we stood to leave, and said, "Wait a minute, we're not done yet." We answered, "Did we miss something?"

He said, "You wrote you'd welcome good-faith discussions about resolving the case." I tried to compose myself without blurting out something I'd later regret. We had just started the case and didn't expect any gestures toward settlement at this early juncture. Yet, here we were. In my biggest demonstration of self-control, I said, "Well, even though it's early, we're always open to talking." We set a mediation date and left the meeting. I was in a state of shock and ran back to my office to contact my client.

After several sessions at mediation, a settlement offer was extended. We discussed the settlement proposal with the client and his mother. The mother, who had a limited education, lived with her son in utter squalor. She was his full-time caregiver, attending to her son's every need, feeding him, bathing him, lifting him into and out of bed, and his battery-powered wheelchair. The wheelchair had broken down, so she had to physically move the chair and her son each and every day.

Above everything else, she had no investment experience and was unreliable during the lawsuit. She insisted she could handle the settlement money being offered. Our duty was to the son, so we filed documents with the court, which had ultimate authority. The judge selected a bank trustee to receive the money and establish a budget for the boy's housing, care, and custody.

The amount of the award guaranteed that there would be funds for my client to receive around-the-clock care in newly renovated housing to accommodate his disability and provide payment for any of his needs over the length of his projected lifetime. The settlement funds he received were deposited with the bank to prevent his mother and his relatives from absconding with the money.

Our judgment was right on target regarding the mother and the boy's absent father's intentions. In addition to dealing with the mother's nefarious intentions, during the mediation sessions, the boy's father, who lived hundreds of miles away, suddenly appeared to provide his opinions as to how the proceeds of the settlement were to be handled. I met with him one time in my office. His only question about any of the proceedings was, "What happens to the money if my son dies?" The question repulsed me, and I never answered. Then I not so politely asked him to leave my office.

A Tale of Two Hips

Implanted medical devices have a long history of improving people's quality of life. Stents can be implanted to restore blocked heart arteries, heart valves can be replaced, and countless other technologies can be utilized to cure ailments and conditions of all types. So, it is with prosthetic devices for knees, hips, and shoulders.

A former client called me from a hospital about her mother. The mother had a hip replacement for a few years before her recent incident. I was told the mother was in the hospital because the hip prosthetic broke inside her, causing her to fall and suffer terrible injuries to her shoulder, face, and body, aside from the broken hip device.

A hip prosthetic comprises a socket that is surgically attached to the pelvis. Then, a ball attached to a pin that is placed, actually hammered, into the hip bone (the femur) that goes into the new prosthetic hip socket. There is a pin that holds the ball and the hip pin together.

In her case, the pin fractured, her leg gave way, and she fell. Aside from her other injuries, removing and replacing the pin was a surgical challenge. Through skillful surgery, the pin was removed and replaced. We resolved the case shortly after

A Tale of Two Hips

filing the lawsuit. In the litigation we learned that the manufacturer's representative is in the operating room, and it's their responsibility to select the appropriate pin size based on the patient's weight and activity level, so they are intimately involved in the hip replacement surgery.

In her case, the pin selected was too thin for her body size and wore out long before its expected usefulness. We negotiated a very sizable settlement, and my client was highly appreciative.

Several years after our case was closed, I received a call from an attorney I knew. He asked if I remembered representing the client, whose hip prosthetic failed. I told him I remembered the case very well. He asked if I still had the file contents, which I did. Then he asked if I would provide my file to him. I told him I could only if the client authorized it. I wondered why he needed it. He told me my former client had called him and retained his firm to file a second claim against the hip prosthetic company because the replacement pin placed in my former client had failed again, and she fell and was injured again. She'd hired them to file the claim. Once again, it proved that neither gratitude nor loyalty exists in some clients, no matter how well you represented them.

Stick to the Law

Usually, except in cases where the attorney has been educated at a "top" law school and gets hired by a big firm, when a lawyer graduates and gets his or her license, they don't know what area they want to practice. After getting my license, I handled cases for a variety of clients in a variety of situations. I took rental evictions, collections, personal injury claims, divorces, criminal cases, and real estate transactions.

A female friend contacted me about her interest in purchasing real estate. She searched in Chicago for a property where she could live and rent apartments for income. We discussed several potential purchases in the weeks and months of her search, and she relied on my judgment and suggestions. I owned my home then and knew the risks and benefits of owning and managing property. Before law school, I had worked in a real estate office, so I was somewhat familiar with the market.

I explained all the pitfalls of owning and managing multifamily property. She must keep accurate records, rent rolls, and operation expenses. She would also be required to handle tenant issues like collecting rent or evicting nonpaying tenants, upkeep in the apartments, refuse removal, and all aspects of the enterprise.

She'd have to hire workmen to maintain the systems in the building and repair or replace the furnace, water heaters, and common areas. I knew she worked and couldn't devote significant time to handle spur-of-the-moment issues that could arise.

I also mentioned that location was crucial for purchasing a property, depending on the viability of the neighborhood. I recommended she buy in an area where her property's value would increase. I recommended a property not subject to heavy traffic or on a busy street.

Finally, armed with all her research and judgment, she bid on a three-flat apartment building, which she was ready to purchase for $127,000. The property needed some updating and improvements, which she could afford to accomplish over time. I prepared the documents, and we closed the transaction without any difficulty.

If I didn't mention it before, she purchased the property in the 3600 block of North Sheffield Avenue! It was directly across the street from Wrigley Field! In the recent past, those properties have been updated and improved, with bleachers on the roofs for spectators of the Cubs games, and the owner of the ball club has purchased most of them for millions of dollars. I don't know if she still owns that property, but I learned to never give real estate advice again.

Job Devotion

I once represented a gentleman who had worked for a chemical company for over thirty years. He'd started as a laborer and worked there so diligently that he received one promotion after another, finally reaching the plant manager position. He was assigned to train the new hires to mix chemicals for the products being produced.

During his career for the company, he had never taken a sick day, had no discipline issues, and only took a two-week vacation, which was part of his compensation package. He never took an extra day off.

The incident that injured him and how I became involved was bizarre. My client was instructing new employees on how to mix chemicals for a flooring application. The drums of chemicals were all clearly marked "Nonflammable." As he demonstrated the procedure, pouring the chemicals into a vat, a powerful blast of flame engulfed him and burned over 27 percent of his body. He was rushed to an area where he was doused with water, wrapped up, and transported to a local hospital. In moments after his evaluation, he was flown by helicopter to a hospital burn unit nearby. He was an inpatient for weeks, wrapped from head to toe in bandages.

Job Devotion

For the uninitiated, burn injuries are horrible. The treatment is worse. Hospital staff must remove the bandages and burned flesh to place new dressings on the injuries, and the process is repeated over and over again until healing starts. Then, the skin grafting can begin. The injuries and the treatment are excruciating. Nerves that are damaged continue to burn the victim.

The client had grafts from his legs attached to his body, arms, and face. It was beyond my comprehension to find the workers' compensation carrier callous and indifferent to this man. They delayed his weekly benefits, denied necessary psychiatric counseling, refused to pay for reasonable and necessary medical expenses, and disrespected him as if any of his injuries or complaints were fabricated. They couldn't care less that he had devoted his entire adult life to the company where he was injured.

When we presented the case to the arbitrator, the company and its insurance carrier were penalized and required to pay total damages for all his injuries. To my astonishment, after he was fully healed and allowed to return to work, he resumed his work with that company until his eventual retirement.

Fighting over Doilies

The most bizarre divorce case I ever handled was a fight between two middle-aged, constantly bickering husband and wife. They had no children and no significant marital property. Each had their own businesses and was doing well, except in the marriage. They had been married in their early forties and lived together for nearly ten years but never really participated in a traditional marriage. They each had their own group of friends, traveled separately, and had different interests. He had a business in which he was thoroughly involved, and she had a separate company. Both had separate bank accounts and separate investments. Each had separate telephone numbers. They owned their vehicles, and except for the marriage license, they were strangers in every aspect of life.

The husband came to my office to discuss filing the divorce complaint and related all the above. The only issue in the marriage was the division of the marital property. Apparently, each spouse came into the marriage with particular personal property, and they couldn't agree on who brought what property into the marriage. They had now

Fighting over Doilies

moved into separate apartments, and each claimed the other had taken property not belonging to the other.

In assessing the disputed situation, I had second thoughts about becoming involved, but to my underestimation; I thought it couldn't be that difficult of a problem if it only involved property. So, I agreed to represent the husband. We filed the complaint, and the wife hired an attorney. I told my client to go through his apartment and make an itemized list of all the property he claimed he brought into the marriage, including a description of each item, where he got it, what he paid for it, and even photographs of the claimed property. My opponent told his client to do the same. Once we had each party's list, we would try to reach common ground. The property would be itemized in a written agreement, and the parties would make the necessary exchanges, if any, and then the divorce would be finalized.

In a few months, the lists were made, and we met at the courthouse to enter the divorce decree. I recall it was midwinter in Chicago. As a side note, my opponent's offices were about a mile from the courthouse. As the hearing ended, and the mutual agreement was confirmed, my opponent went to retrieve his overcoat and found it had been stolen, requiring him to walk back to his office in the blistering cold without his coat.

The judge heard the evidence, considered the agreed property division, and entered judgment for divorce. Both clients were unhappy but tolerant of the divorce terms and the lists that had been prepared and were now incorporated into the divorce decree. The decree established the parties' rights. Mistaken in the belief that these two adult, educated individuals could accomplish the one remaining task, to deliver the property in their possession that had to be exchanged, I advised my client to contact his now ex-wife and arrange a date and time to exchange the personal property they each had been awarded.

A week or so went by, and I heard nothing. I noticed the weather was deteriorating further. I received a telephone call from my client and could sense a problem. Neither party would go to the other's apartment to deliver and exchange the remaining property.

They had arranged to meet in a parking lot near the airport, where they agreed to a face-to-face exchange. They insisted that each attorney attend to guarantee that the divorce property distribution would be done accurately.

As foolhardy as that plan was, it was made more so because the outside air temperature was five below zero.

Reluctantly, I attended. Each party appeared, parked near each other, got out of their vehicles, and opened the trunks of their cars. If it wasn't so ridiculous, standing there and watching them taking salt and pepper shakers, candle sticks, placemats, and other trinkets and handing them over was maddening. As my fingers and toes were freezing and getting numb by the minute, one of the last few items was doilies, so I said, "This is ridiculous. I'm out." I got into my car and left, never to handle another divorce case.

A Trip to the Dentist

A young college-educated girl came to see me complaining about a dentist. She had an impacted wisdom tooth that had to be removed, and she visited her general dentist for the extraction. She saw me when I needed to be more educated on how many dental subspecialties exist. There are general dentists, periodontists, oral surgeons, endodontists, and more specialties for children. With minimal research, I discovered that the general standard of care was that an oral surgeon should perform wisdom tooth extractions, especially in cases with impacted ones. It may be outside the standard of dental care for a general dentist to attempt to achieve a difficult, impacted wisdom tooth extraction.

My client argued that her general dentist lauded his talent and expertise and said he could perform the extraction without any complications, so she made an appointment for the procedure. Although her impacted wisdom tooth was removed, the general dentist damaged her lingual nerve in the process, and after the procedures, she had no feeling or taste in her tongue.

She wanted to sue the dentist and retained me to represent

her. I filed suit, and the dentist's malpractice insurance carrier hired a nationally known, very prim and proper law firm to defend the case. They filed an answer denying any negligence on the dentist's part, denying my client suffered any injury, vehemently denying her injuries were as bad as she claimed.

In large firms, the investigation, known as discovery, involves answering written questions about the claims and defenses, which are exchanged between the parties. The parties are required to produce documents, and sworn statements of the parties are convened for in-person testimony to learn about their claims and defenses.

My client's testimony was scheduled. She appeared at my office for preparation. She was handsomely dressed for the formal appearance as if we were going to court. The deposition was set in the defense attorney's office.

At the appointed time, she met with me at my office and related all the events leading up to the procedure and her condition. She'd undergone evaluations with other dental specialists who told her she had permanent nerve damage. After the preparation, we walked to the defense firm's offices. The offices were very austere, with wood paneling throughout, and extravagant furnishings. Actual oil paintings on the walls of every office were impressive.

In large firms, junior attorneys usually complete the written discovery and sometimes take the parties' sworn statements.

We waited a while and were offered coffee, water, or a snack, which we both declined. Shortly after that, a young, newly admitted attorney greeted us, wearing a three-piece suit, pocket square, and freshly shined shoes, who was fresh out of law school. He took us into an elaborate conference room with a thirty-foot-long conference table for the testimony. The court reporter was there, ready to transcribe the verbatim testimony. It was imposing.

Then, the attorney removed a yellow writing pad, page

after page of his questions, and a multiple-page outline, which he would use to question my client. He started his examination by asking about her identification, education, job duties, and responsibilities. He then moved on to her visit to the dentist. She talked about the history of her event and how the injury had affected her speech and interfered with her work. The attorney began questioning my client about how the injury had affected her social life.

He took copious notes about each element of her loss, loss of taste, and feeling in her tongue when he asked, "How have these injuries affected your social life?"

She answered, "It has affected every aspect of my life, particularly my intimate relationships."

With that, the attorney's face turned bright red. He lifted his notepad and said haltingly, "I have no further questions. This deposition is over." And he hurried out of the deposition room. The case was settled a week later.

The Powers of Observation

I've always been a litigator. As such, I've been responsible for preparing witnesses for their depositions. A deposition is a sworn statement taken by the opponent's attorney. It is usually conducted in an office setting, with the plaintiff being asked questions about their background, education, work experiences, and details about their medical and health condition before and after the incident that caused their injuries.

When it comes time for them to relate how their accident happened, it isn't uncommon for people to be less than entirely accurate in their responses. Sometimes, that is due to unfamiliarity with the deposition process, intimidation, or inaccurate or incomplete recollection. A few examples come to mind.

One witness came in to prepare for his deposition, caused by another vehicle attempting to make a left turn in front of his car. The collision occurred when my client, going straight ahead, collided broadside with the turning vehicle. Extensive damage occurred to my client's vehicle. In the preparation session, he described the damage as being "dents to the bumper and a broken headlight." I then showed him several

The Powers of Observation

photographs I had retrieved from the body shop, which were taken before any work had been done. The images showed the vehicle from all sides and the interior of my client's car. The first thing I noticed was the front of the vehicle was missing. The bumper, hood, and engine were gone. The impact pushed the engine into the passenger compartment. It was demolished. But to him, the bumper and headlight were damaged.

Another client had similar inaccuracies in describing time, speed, and distance. She claimed that she had seen the other vehicle traveling at forty miles per hour. She said when she first saw the other car, it was one foot from her, and if she were to estimate the time it took for the other vehicle to strike her vehicle, it was about a minute.

To demonstrate what a minute was, I had my client watch the wall clock in my office, where I waited until the second hand was at twelve. I said, "Now, watching the clock hand tick off seconds, count for sixty seconds." She watched the secondhand click-off time and how far off her estimate of speed and time was if her timing was accurate. Finally, realizing her mistake, she admitted it was only a few seconds between her seeing the vehicle, the collision, and the distances the cars had traveled.

I always remind clients that when they appear for a deposition, arbitration, or hearing, they should wear appropriate, clean clothing to make a good impression. I represented two men who an uninsured driver had hit, and we had to appear at an arbitration hearing in front of three seasoned, licensed attorneys selected as arbitrators.

Contrary to my instructions, one of the men appeared at my office just a few minutes before the start of the hearing. He wore a soiled T-shirt, which he had stayed the same for days. I couldn't help but notice the image on his T-shirt. It had a car logo on one side of the shirt, and a figure stood beside it. A yellow streak was painted on the shirt, leading from the figure to the logo, indicating the person on the T-shirt was urinating on the logo.

I got up the nerve to ask him, "When you went to select the clothes you would wear to this hearing, is this what you thought was the most appropriate thing you could have chosen?" I couldn't believe his response. "What's wrong with it?" He responded.

A Recipe for Disaster

Ever since childhood, I've been fearful of trains. My uncle worked as a safety supervisor for a railroad for more than fifty years, and he always warned us never to ignore, and faithfully obey crossing gates. He taught us always to be vigilant for trains. He instilled in me a healthy respect for safety, often reinforcing that warning with the fact the trains run on steel tracks and can't stop on a dime. In particular, a freight train traveling sixty miles per hour in a full emergency stop takes a mile to stop.

In recent years, railroads have taken measures to educate the public about the dangers. Still, we often see people driving around lowered crossing gates with flashing lights glaring. The unfortunate outcome is when a train collides with a vehicle, regardless of size. Semi-tractors and trailers become mangled into crumpled metal heaps in a freight train collision.

Around the world, cities have built networks of railroads that serve an essential function. They are a vital part of the economy and serve a significant purpose in hauling freight and passengers. The networks here and abroad enjoy a right-of-way in and around major cities. In those situations, the railroads install fencing and barriers to keep vehicles and pedestrians off their property. Rural areas often have open spaces with no fencing, but the railroads may erect berms or install plantings to thwart inadvertent access to their property.

When fences are placed along a right-of-way, it's incumbent upon the railroad to be vigilant and inspect those fences so as not to allow breaches to occur.

With that background knowledge, I've had to represent victims involved in several incidents involving pedestrians and trains. They aren't pleasant.

One encounter reinforced my uncle's warning well after I became an attorney. A friend and I commuted from our town into the city. The commuter trains were fast, clean, and ran on convenient schedules for both of us.

We used a station on the east side of the two tracks, with parking lots on the east and west sides. Inbound trains ran on the east track and outbound on the west.

At the station house, a pedestrian crossing allowed commuters who parked in the west lot to cross to the east side. The crossing was constructed with railroad ties running across the track area. The ties were coated with a substance that repelled water to protect them from wear. On some early mornings, if there was dew or rain, the water would bead, and the crossing would become slippery. There was a crossing gate, warning bells, and flashing lights as the train approached. On both sides of the intersection, huge signs facing both directions warned not to cross when the signals flashed.

In addition, as the trains approached, there was an audible warning over loudspeakers advising commuters to stand behind the yellow line along the platform as the train entered the station. Most of the commuters were professionals who worked in the downtown area. They all had an abiding respect for the safety rules and warnings. They would be at the station in sufficient time to cross the tracks and go into the station house for coffee and the morning paper—all but one.

A Recipe for Disaster

One commuter had a habit of not arriving on time. Almost every day, as a matter of course, he'd park his car in the west side parking lot and then hurriedly walk toward the pedestrian crossing, ignoring the flashing lights and bells, then raise the gate and sneak across to the east platform as the train approached. No one ever commented, except to themselves, that this educated individual was oblivious to the risks of his behavior.

One morning, a confluence of circumstances joined, and a near disaster occurred. The day was misty, there was moisture on the crossing, the traveler was later than usual, and he was running toward the crossing. The gates had been down, the bells clanging, and lights flashed. The train engine had reached the north end of the platform, about two hundred feet from the pedestrian crossing. As the reckless commuter's foot landed on the crossing, he slipped and fell directly between the tracks, on his back, and could not move. All the commuters were screaming at him to get up, but he was frozen in panic. Seeing this unfold, the engineer attempted to brake for the emergency before him and sounded a horn blast that frightened everyone. The train stopped less than a car length from the guy lying there.

The conductor got off the train, had a few salty words for the commuter, would not let him on the train, and filled out an incident report, which delayed everyone.

We heard that the next day, when the man showed up on time and parked his car on the east lot, the commuters verbally chastised him as a group for putting all of us through such a traumatic and what could have been a deadly event.

That event visibly shook my friend and me. My heart was pounding out of my chest all the way downtown. I could hardly breathe; it was so upsetting. We got up the nerve to take the train a few more times, but the memory of that episode was so disturbing we started sharing the driving downtown and did that for years.

Leo Bleiman

To this day, I vividly recall those images whenever I take the train.

Not Mr. Clean

Industrial accidents occur under bizarre circumstances, and none was more unbelievable than one I was called upon to prosecute for a gentleman working for a company manufacturing potato chips. The plant was in a warehouse that was more than a block long. At the west end were the company's offices. My client worked on a machine at the far, east end of the plant. The din of the machines was deafening, and they ran 24/7/365.

His job was to feed potatoes into the machine. The machine had a "pinch point" where two rollers were about an inch apart. My client would place the potatoes against the moving rollers, squeezing them and pushing them along the conveyers into position to be sliced and cooked.

Raw potatoes have a lot of starch in them, and during the workday, a buildup of starch would cover the rollers, requiring the operator to wipe down the rollers and remove the starchy buildup. On the day of his incident, there was an overabundance of starch on the rollers, and my client thought the machine needed to run more efficiently. He didn't want to shut down the production line by shutting the machine off. He wrapped a rag around his hand and wiped off the starchy buildup. This was a dangerous decision, against all safety measures you could imagine. When he started wiping the rollers, the rag became stuck to the rollers and was pulled in between the rollers, along with his hand, and it continued to pull his arm up to his elbow. In a panic and while enduring enormous, excruciating pain, he went to pull his arm out of the machine, entrapping his other arm. The screaming and shrieking could be heard at the offices a block away. A coworker ran to his aid and shut down the machine. Paramedics were called, and my client was taken to a nearby hospital for treatment of his "degloving" injury to both arms.

After he was treated and released from the hospital and the skin grafting, his arms resembled a skeleton with no muscle structure.

In a workplace setting, even a self-inflicted, horrible decision in the course and scope of one's employment would be covered for benefits. We filed a claim, and my client received his weekly benefits while he was off work, under the care of his physicians, and all his medical care was also covered. I had difficulty convincing him that he was entitled to recover a permanent partial disability or disfigurement award from the arbitrator hearing his case. He was also resistant to offered, psychological counseling to deal with the after-effects of the horrendous scarring. He strenuously resisted claiming those benefits, but eventually accepted an award and signed settlement papers.

The remarkable outcome of the case was his determination to be able to return to work within ninety days of his injury, despite his doctor's warning to wait six months or more for all his injuries to heal properly. He started wearing specially made arm sleeves to hide and reduce the scarring, and he resumed his job as a "feeder," never to try cleaning the rollers while the machine was on ever again.

No Barrel of Fun

Municipalities and park districts have certain legal immunities from suit. A person injured on their property can't just claim the entity was negligent in operating its facilities. The proof usually must show the organization's conduct was willful and conducted with a knowing, reckless disregard for safety, almost to the point of intentionally harming an individual. This is a very high and difficult standard to meet.

A friend called me to report that his ten-year-old nephew had been injured in a park. The Park was conceived, planned, and erected as a community park for children twelve and younger. It had a soft, spongy surface, with the usual recreational equipment in any park. It had swings and slides, seesaws, a small climbing rock, and a sandbox with a device children could sit on and manually operate a shovel to move the sand from place to place.

There was another piece of equipment in the park in the shape of a barrel. It was a popular device with an attractive, circus-like mural on the side. The barrel had a rotating interior, so a child could climb inside the barrel and walk on the rotating part, like a chipmunk wheel. There weren't any signs or warnings on the barrel or the device.

The day of the incident, the nephew went to the park and was using the park equipment until he decided he'd try out the barrel, and he started slowly, rolling the interior around and around. When he began using the device, a couple of much older boys, around thirteen or fourteen, noticed the barrel, and they decided to have fun. They entered the barrel while the nephew was in it and started to spin the barrel at the fastest rate it would go. The nephew couldn't maintain his balance, and he was ejected forcefully out of the barrel, landing on his arm, and suffered a compound fracture. Paramedics were called, and he was taken to an orthopedic surgical center, where the fracture was repaired.

My friend asked me to investigate if a possible claim could be made against the park district or the manufacturer of the barrel ride.

I met with the parents about a week after the incident and surgery, and the boy was in obvious pain. His plans for the summer were dashed, and his rehabilitation was scheduled to take at least three months, including extensive physical therapy after the surgical repair healed. They hired me to represent them as the parents of the injured boy.

My first instinct was to visit the park in person. The signage indicated that the park was designed for children my client's age, not teens. I photographed the barrel from all sides, and the signage indicated that the device was for one person at a time.

I also researched the barrel device to see if other similar claims against the manufacturer or recall notices existed. I retrieved documentation about similar claims and other lawsuits in our state and other states and sent a notice to the manufacturer.

The manufacturer removed the barrel from the park within a week of my letter, which was reported to me by the parents. I was thankful I had taken the photographs. In my searches, I discovered that the manufacturer discontinued manufacturing the barrels. In the law, post-occurrence changes or modifications cannot be used as proof of negligence. However, it indicates control of the device and the premises.

After producing the photographs and the medical documentation, we convinced the manufacturer's counsel that the device was inherently unsafe; it was considered an "attractive nuisance" to children attempting to use it without adequate warnings. The wheel had no monitor to control the rotation speed, and the age limit for children needed to be posted adequately.

The settlement was achieved after hard-fought litigation produced disclosures of prior occurrences, which constituted notice to the manufacturer of the danger the barrel posed for innocent users.

Recovery for a child who becomes injured and whose claim is resolved must be handled in a particular manner. Suppose the recovery is over a certain amount. In that case, the settlement of the claim for the child must be presented to a judge in the court's probate division, where a judge determines if the settlement of the claim is fair and reasonable.

Once approved, the money must be deposited into an account in the child's name and held subject to any further orders of the court or the child reaches eighteen years of age, the age of majority. Many of my former clients whose children had injuries and settlements often objected to that process. I sometimes feared that the parents of some minors would abscond with the money. In the nephew's case, we explained the process and deposited the funds. When the child reached eighteen, he contacted me, and I instructed him how to retrieve the money and put it into his name. I recall this episode because an interesting, unexpected event occurred when we presented our petition to change the name on the account to the probate judge.

Immediately before our case was called, with my clients, their son, and me waiting for the proceedings to start, a sheriff came into the courtroom with a woman in handcuffs. The judge asked, "Do you know why you're here?"

The woman answered, "Yes, I do."

The judge asked, "Where's your son's money?" The woman responded, "I spent it," in a resentful, hostile, and aggressive manner. The judge said: "Take her away," The sheriff placed the woman in a cell next to the courtroom.

Our case was next, and the judge approved the settlement without incident. We were still in the courtroom, writing orders, when the woman was brought back into the room.

The judge said, "You have twenty-four hours to produce all the money you used, or you'll be spending the next few years in jail."

After that demonstration, I knew my clients wouldn't try to use the son's money. Whenever I settle a minor's case, I notify the parents of that incident, stressing that the funds are the child's, not theirs.

Trial Intangibles

Sometimes, experience dictates whether to proceed with a jury trial. Each witness is scrutinized by the twelve jurors, who must be persuaded as to each element of the plaintiff's claim for fault to be decided, as well as the damages and injuries claimed. Jury verdicts require unanimous agreement among all the jurors. If one juror objects and won't agree to the decision of the remaining jurors, it's referred to as a hung jury, and the entire trial proceedings are negated, requiring the parties to conduct a new trial with a new jury.

Complicating those considerations is the ability of the plaintiff and any witnesses to convince the jurors of the truth and accuracy of the testimony and the credibility or believability of those witnesses. It's a very subjective enterprise. The best preparation of a witness won't carry the day if the jury doesn't believe the words coming out of their mouths.

In a diverse population, when people from all walks of life, different backgrounds, and different ethnicities come to court, juries scrutinize everything they say.

This is especially true when dealing with clients whose

native language isn't English. In those cases, it is problematic to delude oneself that their halting use of English words will be well accepted by a jury, even the most open-minded ones. Juries expect claimants to testify truthfully in English. For example, in a person who testifies in Spanish through an interpreter, describing their pain, suffering, or disability comes across as bland and unpersuasive.

Under dire circumstances, I've had clients who had to testify through an interpreter. Qualified interpreters make a significant income in litigation since they usually must be present for the entire trial, interpreting during the testimony of the primary witnesses and, later, at the counsel's table, interpreting the proceedings for the client.

The quality of the interpreter is also vital in the process. At a jury trial, with an interpreter or English speaker, a certified shorthand reporter takes down the testimony in real time. Everything anyone says on the record is typed into a stenographic machine and later put into booklet form. These are general observations from someone who's been through those types of proceedings.

I preface my comments by saying I bear no malice toward any particular language or ethnicity. I've found that many people are distrustful of attorneys. In my experience, more than once, a Polish client of mine has hired and brought their interpreter to depositions and trial hearings, even though I've retained a professional interpreter for the hearing.

Invariably, those clients are fluent in Polish, as are both interpreters. During the questioning, the client chastised the interpreter I hired and the interpreter the client brought, and it became a knockdown, dragged-out brawl, each accusing the other of misstating what the client said.

A Spanish-speaking gentleman claimed to be a professional interpreter. He often appeared at work injury arbitration hearings and was available to interpret for an hourly fee. The claimant's bar recognized his talent well.

Trial Intangibles

Official interpreters are sworn under oath to interpret verbatim from one language to another.

This interpreter was well-experienced in litigated matters. He often translated rather than interpreted, giving his self-edited version of what the witness "meant" to say. He did so with great skill and clarity, and his reputation for winning cases that otherwise would have been lost was legendary.

In other circumstances, a Greek immigrant client I defended was embroiled in a heated divorce proceeding. Every time we appeared in court, the soon-to-be ex-wife, fluent in Greek, ridiculed the interpreter we hired and called her out during the testimony, explaining to the judge that the interpretation was incorrect, false, or inaccurate.

Lastly, there are native English-speaking clients whose educational limitations impacted their ability to convey their thoughts.

In describing the injuries to his knees, one fellow testified that he injured the "cartridges" in his knees in the accident.

Another client whose child was injured came to my office to prepare the settlement documents. I had asked her to bring the birth records for her child to present to the judge so he could appoint her as the legal guardian.

She told me she couldn't find the "bird significant" and would have to get a copy of the document from the hospital where the child was born.

CREDIT CARD SCAM

It's legendary how the lure of money can corrupt even those who aren't needy. An elderly lady came to see me and started sobbing as soon as she sat in my office. She was inconsolable. It took her almost half an hour to calm herself down. When she began to speak, it was apparent she'd been through the trauma of unspeakable dimension, a survivor of the Holocaust; she talked with a hefty accent.

Her story wasn't about her childhood experiences; it involved her son. This lady had always been proud of her achievements and lived with understated dignity. She was well-dressed, well-groomed, and meticulous in explaining her situation. She reached into her purse and produced dozens of documents about her credit reports and delinquency claims against her. She claimed she never owned a credit card and always paid her bills on time, in total, and with checks or cash. Her credit rating had always been perfect and reflected good practices.

Her son was a professional with an active practice. He lived in a very fancy neighborhood on the Pacific Ocean. He drove costly vehicles and was a member of several country clubs. He made a tremendous living, and his lifestyle was such.

Credit Card Scam

When she explained her problem, the situation was easy to understand. The lady's son was living well above his means, as abundant as his income was. He spent thousands monthly, but his cash flow didn't meet his expenses.

His mother, now my client, had saved her entire life from her earnings and had an exemplary credit rating. Her son, not so.

We discovered that the son—armed with my client's Social Security number, birth date, address, phone number, and email address—applied for numerous credit cards in his mother's name but at his residence address. My client learned about the bad credit reports and collection efforts being waged against her through unusual circumstances. Her son stopped paying on those credit accounts. The credit agency tracked her down at her local address, and her son's activities were revealed.

The lady came to me to straighten out the mess caused by her selfish, irresponsible, greedy son. When I became involved, credit purchases were handled much differently than they are today. In the early days of credit card usage, stores that honored cards had a machine to imprint the card on a three-part sales slip that would be placed into a device equipped with a slide. The credit card would be placed in the machine under the sales slip, and the slide would be run across the card and sales slip. The device would create an imprint on the purchase receipt. One copy would be for the merchant, one for the customer, and one for the credit card company. The customer would then sign the sales receipt.

After I placed the credit card companies on notice of our complaint against them, I requested copies of the charge slips the credit card company claimed she signed for.

After several weeks, the companies admitted they couldn't produce sales slips with my client's signature. They all had forged signatures, which the client's son had signed. As her attorney, I had to assert her claim as well as a defense to the charges and had difficulty convincing her to join him in the lawsuit with the credit card companies. She resisted my advice and didn't wish to involve her son. I spent many hours of telephone calls to finally convince her that her son was a necessary party to this dispute. She eventually understood his actions were illegal and reluctantly allowed me to file papers to join her son in the suit.

He had no defense to our claim, exposing his fraud. He had to admit his actions and was forced to pay tens of thousands of dollars of charges he incurred.

Of all the astonishing reactions, my client openly wept when he had to reimburse the credit card companies.

The son never apologized for taking advantage of his mother's good credit and resented me for presenting the claim. Her creditworthiness was reinstated, unblemished by the son's improper conduct.

PICTURES NEVER LIE?

M odern technology, particularly the availability of cell phones and video surveillance, has materially and significantly changed civil litigation. Whether you're aware or not, everything is on video in some form or another, whether it's a store parking lot, public buses and trains, or rural highways. The chance of having someone record an event, intentionally or inadvertently, is significant.

Insurance carriers often hire private investigators to follow injured individuals after a claim has been filed to reveal whether the claimed injuries are valid or exaggerated. Insurance investigators are routinely skeptical of back injury claims.

A client suffered a severe, debilitating low-back injury while working for a car manufacturer. He'd undergone back surgery, which didn't heal, a condition referred to as a nonunion. That's where the bones don't heal, and scar tissue forms. Many nonunions require additional surgery, which was my client's situation. After the second surgery, he was enrolled in extensive physical therapy and took massive amounts of pain medication.

His daily regimen was very restricted. He'd get up, put on

a back brace, take his medication, sleep, go to therapy three to four times a week, and visit with his surgeon every month or two. The defendant's insurance carrier hired a video surveillance team to follow my client. The investigators drove a van with one-way windows and set up their video cameras a block from his house.

For months, they parked their van every day and started taking videos of his every activity. They'd follow him from his house to therapy, then from the therapist to home. On doctor's visit days, the routine was repeated.

I issued a subpoena against the videographer. The notes he prepared revealed his frustration with this assignment. My client was doing everything his doctor and therapist had ordered. He wasn't malingering or demonstrating activities other than those that addressed his care, treatment, and recovery. This frustrated the investigator, who was eager to "catch" my client doing something contradictory to his claim.

At one point, the videographer requested direction from the company on whether to abandon the surveillance. I discovered a note from the investigating company, which directed the videographer to tweak the investigation.

One night, the videographer snuck up to my client's house, took the garbage cans, and dumped their contents all over the front lawn.

The following day, the videographer turned on his cameras to record my client painfully and methodically bending over to pick up the garbage.

When those revelations came out, and we presented the evidence of wrongdoing, the insurance carrier terminated the surveillance and paid us the total injury claim value. After that experience, I always alerted my clients to be aware of circumstances that might seem unusual as they recovered from injuries.

One lady who'd suffered a devastating back injury for which she needed four separate surgeries reported that she'd been noticing a white van parked near her house for weeks. The van had painted windows, was always parked in the exact location, didn't belong to any of her neighbors, and seemed out of place in her neighborhood. Following my advice, she strictly complied with the doctor's orders, assuming she was being watched.

On a brutally hot summer day, she believed a video investigator probably occupied the van. As the compassionate person she'd been, she prepared a pitcher of lemonade and took it and several plastic glasses to the van. She knocked on the driver's door and asked the person inside if they wanted refreshments. Sheepishly, the investigator opened the door. He was dripping with sweat. Very appreciatively, he thanked my client, took the drinks, and shortly after that, drove away, never to be seen again.

Stopping a Bad Guy with a Gun

After I became an attorney, my wife and I bought a small house. It was in a sleepy, suburban town populated by families with small children. Occasionally, we hired a local high school girl to sit with our boys while we went for dinner or to a movie. The house had a small addition on the back that we converted into a family room, with windows and sliding glass doors to the backyard.

We usually went to a local restaurant for dinner, a short drive from home. It was unusual for our sitter ever to call us. We were out one night when our babysitter frantically called us to come home immediately. She was shaking with fear and screaming for us to return. We drove home in a panic, ignoring speed limits or stop signs, not knowing what could have happened. Was it one of our boys? Was it something that happened in the house? We had no idea; we were racing home.

When we arrived home, a police car with flashing lights was in front of our house, and two gigantic officers were walking into it. We raced inside.

We were met by our babysitter, who was crying hysterically. We all tried to calm her down, and the police started questioning her. She said the boys were asleep in their rooms. She was sitting in the back room of the house, watching television, when two or three explosions shattered the room's back window directly behind her. She ran into the house and smartly called the police and then us.

The officers went into the backyard and looked at the windows, which, thankfully, were double-paneled sliding glass doors. The doors were shattered, and glass from the outer layer lay on the grass. Thankfully, the inside window had not been penetrated.

When the police looked at the damage to the windows, they noticed two or three small circular holes in the outer glass. They looked down below the shattered windows and retrieved several shell casings. Then, they walked to the back of the property, where a wooden fence was across the yard. They found several holes in the fence, about waist-high.

Then, the officers walked around the block to the house immediately behind ours and knocked on the door.

The homeowner came and opened the door and identified himself to the officers. The officers told us of the conversation that ensued.

The officer asked, "Do you own this house?" He answered, "Yes."

The officer asked, "Do you own a gun?" He answered, "Yes."

The officer asked, "Did you shoot your gun tonight?" He answered, "Yes.'

The officer said, "Turn over your gun. You're under arrest."

That probably was the shortest police investigation in our town's history. The officers went to the backyard of the shooter's house. Posted on his wooden fence was a target with three bullet holes in it. They took down the target and informed him that his target practice violated several ordinances. His stupidity almost injured and might have killed our babysitter had it not been for the double-paneled sliding glass doors in our back room.

Unbelievably, the shooter's defense was that the paper target and wooden fence should have stopped the bullets from going through the wall.

The shooter was placed on probation, ordered to pay for the replacement of our glass doors, a fine for the ordinance violations, and his gun was confiscated and destroyed. From time to time after that experience, our babysitter continued to stay with our boys, but she never sat and watched television in our back room after that.

Memorable Clashes

No Progress Call

The circuit court of Cook County is one of the busiest court systems in the country. The sheer volume of cases and the number of courtrooms and judges hearing cases is enormous. As cases proceed through the litigation process, from time to time, they can become stalled for any number of reasons. In some circumstances, after a case has been filed, the efforts made to serve the defendant become stalled. The defendant may have moved or can't be found after the sheriff's attempts and steps that have been unsuccessful.

Years ago, a courtroom was arranged to check on the status of service of process, they called it the "no progress" court. The judge assigned to preside over that call was retiring soon, and the process became a routine of continuances, entering orders for additional summons' to be issued, or particular process servers were appointed to skip trace the defendants and serve them. These were purely ministerial matters, which required little effort or attention.

A case came up before the "no progress" judge. Two lawyers appeared; one argued that the defendant had been appropriately served, and a defense attorney was there to say that the service was improper. He argued that the judge should prevent the plaintiff from moving forward with the case. Both attorneys were armed with legal pleadings, filled with arguments of their respective positions.

The arguments went back and forth for nearly an hour and became heated while other attorneys stood around trying to get their continuances and leave to attend to their other cases. After listening intently to both sides, the judge shuffled through the various papers, gathered them up in his hands, handed all the documents back to the attorneys, and said, "Look, guys, I've heard all your arguments, and what I think you should do is take this case back to the supervising judge and have it assigned to a real judge." All true.

Please State Your Name

A personal injury case filed in court involves filing a complaint, service of the suit papers on the defendant, and a process known as discovery. Each side is entitled to serve the other with written questions and requests to produce documents so each side knows what the plaintiff is claiming and what defenses the defendant will raise.

Another part of that process is the taking of depositions and sworn statements of the parties. The court rules provide a deposition time limit of three hours for each side. I represented a young man who sued for personal injuries, and after all the written discovery had been completed, the defense attorney scheduled my client's deposition. I prepared him beforehand on the purpose of the deposition, reviewed his answers to the written materials, and reviewed the type of questions he might be asked. The cardinal rule for a witness being presented for a deposition is to "listen to the question" and "just answer the question being asked." My client was prepared accordingly, and we walked over to the defense lawyer's office. In my experience with most car accident cases, the usual deposition in an accident case lasts no more than an hour. The attorney for the defendant takes a statement of the plaintiff 's background, employment, education, accident facts, medical treatment, and current condition.

We sat down. My client, the plaintiff, was sworn in, and the questioning began. "Please state your full name," he asked. "My name is Leonard L. Lee." (I have changed his name for privacy considerations.) "Have you been known by any other names?"

"Yes."

"What other names have you been known by?" "Lee Leonard is my initials," he said.

"What does the L stand for?" the counsel asked. "Leonard."

"So, is your name Leonard Leonard Lee?"

"No. My name is Leonard L. Lee. Lee is my middle name."

"So, your name is Leonard Lee Lee?" "No. Lee Leonard."

"What do people call you?" the counsel asked. "Lee."

At this point, I said, "Counsel, I know you can ask as many questions as you see fit, and you have three hours, but it's been ten minutes into the deposition, already, so can we just move on beyond the name?" It didn't get much better than that—the life of a lawyer in the big city.

Motion Call Mayhem

The court system I worked in had numerous divisions, and different courtrooms served different purposes. Jury trial rooms heard contested matters. There were chancery courtrooms, which handled nonjury issues, foreclosures, and other things. Eviction courts handled rent cases. One of the courtrooms was for contract cases, which had a gross value of less than $15,000, and the judge presiding over that courtroom for dozens of years was an eccentric fellow nearing retirement age. He stood a little shy of five feet tall, had a rounded physique, was bald, and was always a little late and high-strung, especially at the beginning of the call in his courtroom. The courtroom was ceremonial and had at least fifteen pews on each side of a long aisle. The daily court call always had a high volume of cases. On this particular day, at least fifty lawyers were present, all anxious to hear their cases and move to their other matters. The judge came out later than usual, agitated, and was animated and anxious to get the call of cases done and leave. He hopped up on the bench and sat down, and the first case was called. A cute young female attorney handed up some papers to the judge.

Very impatiently, he asked: "What have you got here?"

She reached up to the bench to retrieve the papers she had just handed him, which agitated him even more, and she started to fumble through them.

"I'm not sure, Your Honor," she said nervously.

The judge snatched the papers from her and started riffling through them himself. "Is it for a default? Is it to file an appearance? Is it to quash service?" he pressed. "I don't know, Your Honor. Maybe if I looked more carefully, I could tell you." Then the judge said out loud in a booming rebuke, which everyone in the courtroom could hear,

"Well, if you don't know, HOW THE FUCK AM I SUPPOSED TO KNOW?"

The roar from the assembled crowd was deafening. And the judge excused himself and returned to his chambers until the laughter died.

This judge's courtroom had a small powder room adjacent to the courtroom. I learned from a fellow attorney, that on one occasion, he was in the middle of arguing a dispositive motion with another attorney. They were in a heated argument, which was going on with back and forth statements. The judge was agitated. He said, "Look, guys, I don't want to cut either of you off, but I have to use the bathroom very badly, I'm going to go into the bathroom, and I'll leave the door open, so I can hear both of you, and you go on with your arguments, and I'll hear you from there." Whereupon, he did just that, and not only did HE hear them, the attorneys Heard HIM!!!!

LOCAL LAW

A noticeable difference exists between appearing in your local jurisdiction and the treatment you get if you travel to other counties. You become familiar with the judges in your district by appearing and arguing cases before them, and you gain a certain amount of credibility over time. That is lost where you're not known and unfamiliar with the local judges or rules.

Familiarity with the judges you often appear before serves you well, mainly when you are relying somewhat on your reputation with a judge who can exercise their discretion one way or the other. A former client of mine had moved away and relocated to a small town in Western Illinois. He called me with a request to handle a personal injury claim. I was reluctant to consider taking his case due to the distance I would need to travel, if the case had to be filed in the local court system. My client knew I'd be an"outsider", but he wanted me to represent him.

The facts he recounted involved an injury from a bar fight. He had been in a local bar, minding his own business, watching a ball game, when he suffered a broken nose through no fault of his own. He was sitting at the bar, and two drunk (in legal terms, overserved) patrons became entangled in a fistfight, and an accidental punch hit my former client in the face, breaking his nose. He received medical care and had no health insurance, so we had to file suit.

There is a law that applies to bar owners. Suppose a patron is "overserved" alcohol and becomes intoxicated. In that case, the bar owner can be liable for damages if the intoxicated patron injures a third party, which was my client's situation. I took the case, and despite my most diligent efforts, we could not achieve a settlement of the case. I filed a lawsuit against the bar owner, and we completed the pretrial discovery matters. After that, to my surprise, the defendant's attorney suggested we ask the presiding judge to conduct a pretrial conference to see if we could narrow the issues for trial and discuss the possibility of settling the case in its entirety.

The courthouse was located eighty miles from my home. I left my house around 6:00 a.m. to ensure I arrived in plenty of time for the pretrial conference scheduled for 9:00 a.m. The night before, I reviewed all my file documents, legal precedents, photographs of my client's injured face, medical bills, and a synopsis of the issues I intended to argue at the conference.

I arrived well before the meeting in very conservative attire (a three-piece suit, a monochromatic tie, and polished shoes) and my well-organized file. I was ready for trial if it came to that. When I arrived, the bailiff greeted me, asked for my name and what case I had on the court call, and told me to sit in the small rural courtroom, one of only three in the entire courthouse. While seated there, I could hear a conversation and loud laughter from the chambers behind the courtroom wall. After a while, the bailiff came out of the chambers to usher me in the back. To my surprise, the opposing attorney, a few other lawyers, and the judge were seated around a conference table and were having coffee.

The judge beckoned me to sit next to the opposing

attorney and introduced the people in the room. "Have you met Buddy?" he asked, referring to my opponent. He quickly corrected himself, "I mean the counsel." And he gave his name. "Introduce yourself, Counsel," to which I responded. The others in the room were likewise introduced.

"We were just discussing the bash we had last night at the country club, so don't mind us," the judge said.

"What kind of case do you have here?" the judge asked.

"It's a dram shop case, Judge," I responded.

"Oh," he said.

"Buddy, would you and Shorty and Chucky [not their real names] mind stepping out to the courtroom for a minute while I converse with the counsel here and get to know the plaintiff's attorney?" the judge said.

"Sure, no problem," said Buddy. They all left. They were looking at me like a lamb being led to the slaughterhouse.

Once he left, the judge turned to me.

He began, "You're not from around here, are you?" He knew I wasn't. "You know, Counsel," he continued, "let me give you a little background about our town." "This here is a small town. Everybody knows everybody. The locals all work in the town. They all go to the same church, shop at the same stores, and the social scene is the tavern where this fight took place. The businesses get their entire income from the local population." I sensed this was not just random information about commerce.

He continued, "The bars and restaurants are the lifeblood of this community [or words to that effect]." He emphasized the lifeblood reference. "So, if this case goes to trial, the whole jury pool will be made up of our people who have been to that bar, who know the bar owner, know each other, may know your client, and probably know me. We all feel bad that your guy was an innocent bystander to this brawl and that he got hurt," he voiced his sympathy.

"But, you know," he continued, "we don't like to punish the bars around here." At this point, I was not receiving helpful or unbiased information from the person ruling on the issues in the case. I didn't need to be hit over the head with a baseball bat to understand the underlying message.

"Now, before you arrived, I reviewed the file," the judge continued, "and I had a brief conversation about the case with Buddy, the opposing counsel. The message I received is that—and I'm not speaking for him—if he were able to convince his principal to pay you [at which point he provided a figure that was equal to the medical bills my client had received], I'd recommend that figure to you, to resolve this case. I think that if that figure was offered, it would be fair and reasonable."

After listening to him and digesting the scenario I had just witnessed, I said, "Well, Judge, if you think that's a fair figure, my client would be an utter fool to reject that offer." I had authority from my client to accept any offer to avoid a trial, so I told the judge I'd take that proposal. I thanked him for his "effort" in resolving the case, prepared an order, and left the courtroom and that county, vowing never to handle another matter in a foreign county unless I referred the case to a local attorney.

No Green Card

An attorney must represent his client faithfully. When a conflict arises between the lawyer and the client, which causes the irretrievable breakdown of their trust and confidence, the attorney must withdraw from the representation upon notice so that the client can have an opportunity to retain an attorney to replace prior counsel.

Such was the situation, when I was handling a motor vehicle collision with a client I had investigated and prosecuted. She had been the victim of a rear-end collision, after which a hospital emergency department treated her. After outpatient care, she was treated for several weeks for soft-tissue muscle injuries and released from care. The client worked a block from my office, and her employment had disability benefits, which she used while being treated for her injuries. After her discharge from care, she continued to receive disability benefits from her employer for over a year. She wanted to receive payment for that lost time, even though she was paid benefits for her lost time from work.

When a person is injured and presents a claim, including claims for lost wages, there must be proof that all the care, treatment, and loss of work were causally related to the initial collision. It became clear that the insurance carrier for the at-fault party would not accept more than a year's worth of lostwages and would not consider the time the client lost after her discharge from her treatment and attending physician.

When I explained the problem, my client took offense, claiming she was still in pain and unable to work even though she wasn't seeing any doctor or therapist.

We had numerous discussions, after which I explained a settlement offer was made, which did not include any funds for the disputed lost wages. She objected and told me she wanted to retain another lawyer to press her case further to recover her lost wages. One of the conditions of her employer's wage-loss benefit plan required her to pay back any benefits if she collected money from the person who caused the collision.

The case was pending in court, and to formally terminate our attorney-client relationship, I was required to prepare and present a motion to the presiding judge, to formally withdraw as my client's attorney. By rule I had to serve her with the papers, (for due process purposes) and show the service of the papers and the motion to the judge presiding over the case.

I prepared and filed the necessary papers, and since my client worked a block from my office, I hand-delivered the documents to her, in person, and had her sign a receipt showing she had notice of the motion and the hearing date. She consented to my withdrawal.

Notice of the motion is required for due process considerations. There are several methods of proving notice, which can be done by mail, certified mail, or with a return receipt (a green card, which the client must sign acknowledging receipt). Sometimes, a sheriff must deliver the documents to a client and sign an affidavit of service. By rule, the law provides that personal service is the best, incontrovertible service.

On the date of the hearing on the motion, I stepped up

before the judge and announced I was presenting a motion to withdraw.

The judge said, "Where is the green card?"

I responded, "There is no green card. I made service by personally delivering the documents to the client, and she signed for it." I showed her the client's signature on the document. The judge was unimpressed and not persuaded by my statement and indignantly asked, "What does the statute say about service, Counsel?" In a loud voice, she inquired, sending a clear message to the other attorneys seated in the courtroom waiting to present their cases. "Well, Judge," I responded, "the last time I checked, personal service is the best." She replied, "Not in this courtroom."

"Judge, are you saying that personal service is not good service?" I asked. "That's exactly what I'm saying," she responded, emphasizing exactly. So, she stated she would only grant my motion to withdraw if I produced a green card from a certified mail service.

I prepared an order stating, "The motion to withdraw is denied. The court finds personal service is not good service," which I handed to the judge. She took it from me and quickly signed it. I believe she left the bench or was forced to retire shortly after that episode.

Not Guilty—No Divorce

Of all the cases I tried, one of the most memorable was a contested divorce case. It is unique because it started as an uncontested case. My client was the husband. His wife wanted a divorce from him. He initially resigned himself to the breakdown of the marriage. If she wanted out of the marriage, he wouldn't contest it, and he, too, could move on with his life. He had moved out of their house.

The wife had filed her case for divorce based on mental cruelty. In cases where there is an allegation of mental cruelty, the nature and extent of the cognitive and emotional trauma on the suing party requires the testimony of a professional practicing in the field of sociology, psychiatry, or psychology to testify to the elements of the accusations and how the conduct of the offending spouse caused all the mental and emotional symptoms. It is a challenging basis to prove without professional testimony in support of the allegations.

The emotional and mental distress allegations must be based on severe ongoing behavior, manifesting in the victim's fears of dread, doom, and physical and emotional disturbance of the spouse's life.

Before meeting with lawyers, the couple had discussed the property division between themselves. My client wasn't interested in anything in particular. There was furniture, the bric-a-brac, pots, pans, television sets, beds, and kitchen appliances. He couldn't care less about those things and was content to give it all to her to gain his freedom. All he wanted were his clothes, television, and clock radio.

Everything was agreed upon, and my client was satisfied with the terms up to the final day of the case. In anticipation that all the terms were agreed upon, he had already moved out of their house and rented an apartment. He was moving forward, content in the knowledge that he'd soon be a free man.

The parties and the attorneys were ready to proceed with the formal testimony to obtain the divorce and divide the property. We expected a routine prove-up of the allegations in her complaint when the wife brought up a critical issue. She insisted that her husband pay monthly support money for her until she retired from her job, which was several years away.

When the wife's attorney approached us in the rear of the courtroom, I could see the dismay on his face. He said, "My client brought up another issue, and she won't go through with the hearing unless your client agrees to pay maintenance to her until she retires."

I asked, "How much is she asking for?"

"She wants $100 a week." Upon hearing this, my client had a visceral reaction, and I could almost sense his anger and hostility.

I took my client out of the courtroom, and we sat on the benches in the hallway, silently contemplating what had just occurred.

"You know," he started, "I went along with this whole thing because that's what she wanted, and I didn't want to stop her. I knew I'd be just fine living alone."

He continued, "I gave her everything she asked for—the

house, the car, the furniture, and everything else—and now she pulls something like this! Go tell them I'm not agreeing to anything." "Let's go to trial. We'll see what she gets from the judge."

I returned to the courtroom alone and conveyed the news to my opponent. "He's contesting the divorce". "We no longer have a deal and must set the case for trial."

We approached the judge and informed him that the proposed settlement was off, and we needed to set the case for trial as a contested mental cruelty case.

The judge accepted our statements and set the case for trial on a date specific about a month later. I was aware of the judge's reputation in the courthouse since I had other cases before him, and I was aware he was more inclined to favor the husband when exercising his discretion. He was a wild-game hunter and displays in his chambers chronicled a lifetime of safaris. He was a rugged outdoorsman. He was a scion of a business empire and incredibly wealthy. The family had a reputation for requiring any person marrying into it to sign a waiver releasing the family from any potential threats against the family business should trouble arise in a marriage.

In the judge's chambers were buffalo and elk heads on the walls, as well as pictures of him with trophy kills of bears and other creatures. The judge's chambers were a museum of masculinity.

The trial day came, and the wife was called as the one and only witness by her attorney. She testified about her name, age, and the names and ages of her children, who were all grown and out of the house, and she identified the date and place of the marriage.

She discussed the marital property in the house, their bank accounts, her employment, the husband's employment, and the wages they earned. Then, she started to testify about the severe mental and emotional factors that led to her seeking a divorce.

"Whenever my family comes to our house, he goes into his room and closes the door," she started. "He never calls my mother," she added.

"When I ask him what to make for dinner, he tells me, 'Anything you want to make.'" Her attorney asked, "Anything else?"

"No," she answered.

In every case, including divorces, the suing party must meet the burden of proof in their lawsuit. In a civil case, the suing party must present proof, from the evidence, that what they testify about is more probably true than not true.

To prove mental distress, a person must present testimony about the anguish and suffering a person has gone through, which caused the irretrievable breakdown of the marriage and the imperiled mental well-being of the person seeking the divorce.

Unless such proof is given, the opposing party may ask the judge hearing the case to dismiss it because of insufficient proof, which is what I did.

"Your Honor," I said, "I'm moving for a directed finding that the plaintiff has not met her burden of proof, and she is not entitled to a judgment for divorce from my client." The judge said, "I find a wholly insufficient basis in the evidence presented to grant a divorce, and the motion to dismiss is now granted. Write your order."

The wife and her attorney were shell-shocked. My client asked me, "What happened?"

And I explained she didn't provide enough proof to get the divorce.

"What happens now?" he inquired.

"You have your options," I told him. "And you have every right to move back into the house." He moved back into the house the very next day.

I had been waiting to hear from my client or opposing

counsel for three or four months. One morning, I received a telephone call from the opposing counsel. He was desperate.

"Please have your client file for a divorce from my client. She's driving me crazy," he said. She'd called the lawyer daily about my client, how he was still in the house, ignoring her family, and insisted that she needed a divorce.

I called my client and told him about the call and my recommendation of what he could do. We ended up filing for divorce from the wife. We negotiated a settlement of the divorce case, with the division of the property based on an even distribution of all the property, selling the house and dividing the proceeds in half; my client got the newer of the two cars, the more expensive television, and last but not least, no payment of maintenance whatsoever.

My client was ecstatic and a very satisfied ex-husband.

A Slippery Slope

One of my most satisfying cases involved a young man of nineteen years of age who was in a very tragic one-vehicle incident that left him disabled. I'll refer to him as Jose. He was a passenger in a vehicle. The driver lost control and crashed, ejecting Jose from the car. His mother contacted a colleague who didn't prosecute personal injury cases, and we all met to discuss any potential claims we could pursue for the young man. His medical expenses were gigantic and ongoing. The mother provided us with a history of the events and produced a police report regarding the incident.

What was curious about the case and unusual was how the claim had developed before I became involved in the investigation. A second vehicle was traveling alongside the car Jose was in. Both cars were going fast along a roadway when they encountered a commuter railroad crossing, and the vehicle Jose was in lost control and crashed. Within days of the incident, the insurance carriers for both vehicles tendered their insurance policy liability limits. They requested full releases of any liability, which Jose's mother refused to sign.

The policy limits of both cars had less than $50,000 in total coverage.

After we spoke with Jose's mother, I made a copy of the police report and went to the accident scene. I started taking photographs from all the approaches to the area. The weather was mild and clear, and the pavement had no rain or moisture. However, while walking near the railroad crossing, when I stepped on the rubberized material adjacent to the tracks that formed the actual crossing, it was as slippery as ice underfoot. I later learned that oil residue from the trains passing over the crossing left a film or deposit on the rubber material, making it slick as glass.

I reported my findings to my colleague and scheduled a second meeting with Jose's mother. We arranged to meet Jose to discuss my findings and review the pictures. We decided to pursue a claim against the manufacturer of the crossing material. When we usually initiate a claim, we send a letter to the alleged at-fault party, advising them of our representation and a brief description of the basis of our lawsuit, usually alleging they were negligent or their product was defective.

In Jose's case, we notified the railroad and the crossing material manufacturer of our representation of Jose and the nature of our claim.

I will always remember the response we received. Usually, we receive a letter denying any responsibility and advising us that the claim will be referred to the company's insurance carrier. In this case, on the railroad's letterhead, and in the most graphic language I'd ever read, was a scathing denial of liability, along with terminology that accused us of wrongdoing, along the lines of "You lawyers... and your concocted theories of negligence...make me sick... Just because a railroad crossing is within five miles of an accident...right away, you accuse us of wrongdoing." The last part was the kicker: "It will be a cold day in hell before we pay a red cent on this claim."

A Slippery Slope

We commenced the claim accordingly and retained an expert, who went out to the crossing and conducted testing under a theory that the coefficient of friction of the crossing had been affected due to a combination of the residue from the passing trains and the composition of the crossing material. That made the crossing as slippery as ice, even in dry conditions. This was in stark contrast to the roadway pavement next to the crossing, and that contributed to causing Jose's vehicle to spin out of control.

Instead of paying "one red cent," we collected close to a million dollars for Jose. The experience taught me several things which I live by daily. I always try to visit the scene of an occurrence to acquaint myself with the circumstances, the lay of the land, and any tangible evidence I could glean from a personal inspection. That visit handsomely paid off for our client.

Don't Touch Our Sidewalk

When people fall, no matter how serious of an injury they suffer, they face the incredible challenge of collecting from anyone charged with causing the fall in the first place. The law requires a person claiming damages to prove that the person accused of being negligent had a legal duty to the injured person; they breached that duty and the injuries resulted from the negligence. Whether a duty exists is a legal question. A judge determines if a duty exists in the law. The criteria involve several factors and require an analysis of a balancing act of various factors. Did the owner of the property have notice of the hazard? Was the injured person paying attention to where they were walking? Was the alleged "defect" so minor as to constitute an unactionable occurrence (also called the de minimis rule)?

When a municipality is involved, imposing a duty is even more difficult. A municipal entity must maintain its property, streets, sidewalks, and publicly owned property. Illinois has established specific laws that grant municipalities immunity from suits and can raise other defenses. The most common defense to a duty a defendant owes is the concept of notice.

Don't Touch Our Sidewalk

A city must be made aware of a defect on its property before it can be sued. Usually, the person who falls has not notified the municipality; and if they had, then the argument is that they knew about the defect that caused their fall and were not paying attention. Some falls are caused by the injured person not paying attention to an apparent, obvious defect, which they should have avoided. Other defenses arise from the nature of the defect. If it is so minor that it's determined to be de minimis or so small, the municipality can't be liable for such minor defects as actionable. Falls on ice pose another problem with proof of liability since everyone knows icy patches (even black ice) should not be encountered, even if the fall results in fractures or other serious injuries. We've heard of people slipping and falling on slippery surfaces in the lobby of stores and apartment buildings where studies of the coefficient of friction can be measured. The "open and obvious" defense may defeat a claim even then.

Facing those challenges in proofs makes fall-down cases some of the most difficult to win. Even the most creative attorneys need help proving and succeeding in fall-down cases. I represented a beer delivery driver who fell and suffered a severe leg fracture on a city sidewalk. To set the scene, he fell while pushing a two-wheeled metal dolly from his truck to a liquor store customer. His cart had five fully loaded cases on it. He had delivered to this store countless times and was aware of open holes in the sidewalk. Some city sidewalks are built over an open vault next to existing buildings. Maintenance of the sidewalks is the municipality's responsibility. While pushing the loaded cart with the cases in front of him, my client could not navigate around the holes or merely forgot they were there. He tripped in one of the holes, fell to the ground, and suffered a compound leg fracture. He called the paramedics, who took him to a local hospital, where he underwent surgery to repair his leg, placing rods in his leg to assist the healing process. My client had never notified the building owner adjacent to the sidewalk or the city of the sidewalk holes.

As circumstances existed, we filed a lawsuit against the city and the owner of the building adjacent to the sidewalk. Our complaint alleged negligence against the owner for allowing the holes to exist and against the city for failing to repair the sidewalk. The building owner had insurance, and the company tendered the case's defense to the City. The city rejected the tender of defense and raised all the usual defenses to a fall-down case. The city claimed they had no notice of the defect; it was open and obvious, and my client was responsible for not paying attention to the area where he was walking.

It was only luck, and unbeknownst to me, that the building owner also owned a candy store one block from the location of my client's fall on the sidewalk. I had personally visited the candy store from time to time before my client's incident. After I filed our lawsuit, I refused to patronize that store again. When it came time to take the building owner's deposition, he walked into the deposition room, recognized me, and graciously acknowledged me before being sworn in to testify. I found that quite unusual and curious.

The deposition proceeded with me asking the usual background questions to establish his ownership of the building, his responsibility to maintain the structure, his awareness of the holes in the sidewalk, and his awareness that the sidewalk posed a danger to persons walking on it. I then inquired if he had ever notified the city of the condition of the sidewalk, and to my astonishment, he admitted that he had.

"How did you notify the city?" I asked. "I wrote the alderman," he answered.

"How many times did you tell the alderman?" I asked.

The building owner then removed a file folder from his attaché case and showed me several letters from him, addressed to the alderman, over several months, advising thecity of the holes in the sidewalk and warning the city that the holes posed a risk of people injuring themselves if they tripped and fell.

One of the building owner's letters declared, "If you people don't repair the sidewalk, I will hire a contractor of my own to repair it."

The following letter was the blockbuster that resolved the case. The alderman responded in writing to the building owner, warning him that if he did anything to repair the sidewalk, the city would sue him and require him to restore the sidewalk to its original condition (with the holes). At that point, I asked to make duplicate copies of the letters, returned the original letters to the defendant, and gave the corporation counsel a set of documents to bring back to his office. About a week later, I received a substantial offer to settle the case from the city and resolved the case.

In nearly forty years of practice, that was the first and last time I witnessed a municipality settle a fall-down case on a sidewalk. Since the alderman admitted they had notice of the defective condition of the sidewalk, and they paid the total value for the injuries.

Psycho Arbitrator

A woman came into my office with a cast on her leg and a story so convoluted it would take a hundred pages to describe. She was working at a factory and was constantly harassed by her coworkers. She felt discriminated against for not being a "townie," working in a factory where everyone else was related by kinship or neighbors, and the employees were all "against her." I won't recount all the problems she described, except that she fell inside the plant and fractured her leg doing her job. She tried to work with the injury, but it became too complicated, and with the turmoil to which she was being subjected, she decided to file a claim and chose me to represent her. Our first interview took almost two hours because she would break down every few minutes, crying uncontrollably about the injustices she had gone through. Once I had enough information to prepare an application for adjustment of claim, and the other documents necessary to file her case at the Illinois Industrial Commission (the name was changed to the Illinois Workers' Compensation Commission), she regained her composure and started to leave my office.

Then she sat back down and repeated almost every

detailof the harassment and the incident. I realized that this person not only had a physical injury but felt tormented to such a degree that it consumed her. She also told me she had quit her job due to the harassment. It isn't often the case where a physical injury causes a mental breakdown or traumatic neurosis. I sincerely felt that she might be suffering from such an emotional component caused by her injury. I suggested she seek professional counseling. She left my office slightly more composed, and I filed her case to proceed with my investigation.

I subpoenaed her work records, including her health records, from her employer, and when I received them, I noticed that her employer had documented some of her complaints. In my contact with her, she informed me that she was being evaluated and treated for her physical and emotional condition.

The employer's insurance carrier accepted the claim for her injured leg but rejected the emotional element I had presented. With no movement toward a resolution, we set the case for arbitration. The employer retained a psychologist to counter our claim, and I requested my client's treating psychologist appear for the hearing.

The arbitrator for our case had been hearing cases for the better part of forty years. He had always been a little eccentric. He had a water pitcher and a stack of four-ounce water cups on his desk. He had an insatiable thirst, so he'd fill and sip from them several times every minute or two during most hearings that lasted a half hour or more. Since they were so small, he often spilled some water during the refilling process, and he had a stack of paper towels to sop up the spillage in a constant, distracting performance art of insanity. He also had an assigned handwriting shorthand reporter taking down the word-for-word testimony of witnesses. At the time, most court reporters used stenographic machines to record the testimony, but this gentleman was from the old school.

It came time for our case to be heard. Both psychologists testified about their examinations and findings, with our treating and attending doctor identifying the symptoms and the respondent's consultant denying that my client was impaired by the events. At that juncture, the arbitrator spilled water all over his notes and desk, and he adjourned the hearing. At that point, we all exited the courtroom and stood outside while the arbitrator composed himself and cleaned up his desk.

While standing in the hallway, we saw the arbitrator scurrying around, cleaning and mopping his desk. At this point, the two psychologists who had diametrically differed in their analysis of my client's condition both agreed the arbitrator needed intense therapy.

The case outcome became even more confusing, through no fault of anyone. The court reporter who had taken down all the testimony by hand, had a heart attack and suddenly died, leaving his handwritten notes behind. Every handwriting court reporter has shortcuts, but no one could decipher the notes left behind. Eventually, we sat down with the psychologists' reports and settled the case to everyone's satisfaction.

No Good Deed Goes Unpunished

2000 I bought the first edition of an Audi TT sports car. It was a dream car for me. It had gorgeous lines and a high-powered stick shift and was super-fast. When I picked up the vehicle in Wheaton, I drove to I-88, put my foot on the gas, and was doing eighty, which felt like fifty. Cars were moving out of my lane as I whizzed past. I was in car heaven.

A few months after I got the car, one morning, I was smoothly moving in and out of traffic to avoid slower vehicles in "my" lane when I noticed a state trooper directly on my tail, with lights flashing and a spotlight alerting me to pull over. As soon as I got to the shoulder, the officer was out of his car, running toward my car. He was livid and screaming at the top of his lungs. He howled, "Can you tell me why you drove eighty miles an hour, weaving in and out of traffic and endangering everyone?" His face was bright red, and I could see the veins popping in his temple. I immediately sensed his hostility toward me and thought it was a perfect opportunity to inject some fun into the situation. I said, "I'd attribute that behavior as negligent driving." He was not amused. He returned to his cruiser and wrote several traffic violations as slowly as possible. I must have waited half an hour. Then he walked up to the window, threw the citations he'd written at me, and stormed back to his vehicle.

Shortly after that incident, I was retained to represent the family of a young girl killed in a pedestrian/vehicle collision on the I-290 expressway.

The accident was ghastly. The facts were somewhat murky and convoluted. The girl was about twenty-one, and she'd been up at a lake with another girl and a much older gentleman. The man was driving them back to the Chicago area after a day of drinking and who knows what else. She'd gotten intoxicated and fell asleep in the car on the ride home. As they reached the Schaumburg area, while driving in the express lanes on I-290 at nine at night, one of the tires went flat, and the driver pulled the vehicle onto the east shoulder of the express lanes to fix the flat. While he was busy repairing the tire, the girl awoke. She must have been in a stupor, disoriented and confused about what was happening. In an inexplicable and tragic misjudgment, the girl exited the vehicle. She foolishly decided to attempt to cross the expressway, apparently intending to walk to a nearby restaurant to call her parents to pick her up and drive her home. Traffic along that stretch of highway is heavy and nonstop, traveling seventy-five to eighty miles an hour. Remarkably, she crossed almost all the moving lanes of travel and had reached the farthest lane to the west when she was struck by a vehicle, thrown into the air across a median divider, and struck and killed by another car.

I met with the distraught parents. I reviewed their auto liability policy and the detailed police report. Fatal cases are reported in great detail by a major accident investigation unit. The interview was one of the most difficult I'd ever had. The parents brought photographs of the girl and awards she'd received, and they detailed virtually every achievement she'd acquired through her schooling. I prepared a detailed claim to present against the driver of the girl's car and the other two vehicles involved. After resolving many insurances coverage issues, an underinsured motorist arbitration of the case was scheduled.

The main issue in the claim was whether the girl had made it to the "fog line" at the west edge of the express lanes. The "fog line" is a painted stripe with illumination features so vehicles can determine where the highway is divided from the shoulder under poor lighting conditions. If she were west of the fog line, on the shoulder, she would, arguably, have some right to be there, and her presence wouldn't exclude her from recovery. We needed to prove the first striking vehicle had crossed the fog line. Under such facts, she would be considered as, at least, partially protected from legal liability for her negligence; however, if she was struck while on the traveling lanes, her death would wholly be the result of her negligence and a bar to any recovery.

The parents' insurance policy had coverage limits of $ 250,000 for an injury to any one person. We argued if she was across the fog line, she could only be 50 percent of the cause of her death, and we should prevail and collect the $250,000. We discussed the issue with the carrier's attorney and agreed that the arbitrator would determine the percentage of fault. If we proved she was only 50 percent negligent, we'd receive the total policy limits at arbitration. We'd receive zero if the arbitrator determined that she was more than 50 percent liable for causing her death.

The arbitration hearing was emotional and heart-wrenching. The parents testified about their daughter's life, schooling, and recreational activities and dashed hopes for her future. Tears were flowing. We introduced the coroner's report about the cause of death and presented the funeral bills and the bill for the elaborate headstone the parents wanted to place on the girl's grave.

The arbitration was conducted before a retired jurist

respected by both sides of the bar. When we were preparing the case, I knew the critical issue was the fog line. I sent a subpoena for the investigating State of Illinois officer to appear and testify to obtain his opinion about the location of the initial impact. Imagine my utter surprise when the state police officer who appeared was the same officer who had stopped and ticketed me months before. He was as surprised as I was, and he remembered me. At the very least, I had mixed emotions about the turnabout in our roles in this unusual situation. I relied on his sworn oath of office that he'd be truthful in his testimony. He was sworn in, and I qualified him as the investigating officer and walked him through his steps, the measurements he recorded, and the specific details of his report. When the time came, I asked him the critical question, "From your examination of the scene, Officer, was my client's daughter on the shoulder, west of the fog line, when she was initially struck?" He said, "Yes, she was."

I won.

The insurance attorney congratulated me on doing a masterful job under challenging circumstances, and the carrier issued a check for the $250,000 policy limit. A few weeks later, the parents came to my office to distribute the funds. They were so thankful and blessed me for the outstanding work I had done for them and the memory of their daughter. They showed me a picture of the enormous monument they were designing and placing on her grave and, through tears, left my office.

About a year after the case was closed, I was at my desk when my assistant came in and asked me to come out into our lobby. A Cook County sheriff was standing in full uniform, holding some documents. He handed them to me, said, "Consider yourself served," and left.

I leafed through the papers, and to my amazement and considerable resentment, I was reading a legal malpractice complaint the parents had filed against me. The charge was that instead of proceeding with the case they hired me to prosecute, which I won under very tenuous circumstances for the death of their daughter, they claimed I should have filed suit against their insurance carrier to raise the liability limit of their policy. Their automobile liability policy was the same, with the same company and the same coverages, which they'd had renewed repeatedly for many years before the incident involving their daughter. I was outraged. There was no merit whatsoever in the lawsuit.

One of the first paragraphs in an automobile liability policy is a warning to "read your policy." Suppose any of the policy's provisions or the coverage amounts must be corrected. In that case, the customer must contact the company's agent and require a correction. Here, it became evident that the parents' greed overwhelmed their daughter's emotional loss.

It only took a few weeks to file a motion with the court to throw out the complaint, which had no merit whatsoever. That case taught me a critical lesson about gratitude for doing a masterful job.

CONTRITION

A colleague of mine was a real estate lawyer. His entire practice was devoted to selling, purchasing, and developing real estate. That's all he did; he was a genius in his field. He was rumored to read the contract document for each transaction, including the mortgage documents and promissory notes for every deal. That was unparalleled preparation. He routinely did those tasks as part of his usual and customary responsibilities.

Long before becoming an attorney, he had a reputation for being very aggressive. He either began or ended numerous all-out fistfights in his childhood. He had an anger issue, which he tried to temper down in college and law school, sometimes unsuccessfully. He was big and robust and could back up any "threats" that might have originated with him or come his way.

I learned that in college, he rented a second-floor apartment near campus. He and a friend roomed together. They had accumulated a beer can tower along one apartment wall, like a pyramid of achievement. College guys do some crazy stuff.

One afternoon, when the roommates were out at class, the

landlord, exercising his "right" of entry in their lease, unwittingly and not knowing the impending wrath of the tenants, without notice or consent, decided to enter the apartment to "check things out."

To his amazement, my friend arrived while the landlord was in the apartment. At that moment, my friend's lifelong but somewhat controlled vitriol emerged. In a fit of rage, he took the landlord over to the balcony of the apartment, grabbed hold of his ankles, picked him up over the railing, held him dangling by the ankles, and told him, "If you ever come into our apartment again, the next time I'll let go!"

So, it was not against his inborn nature to engage in angry outbursts from time to time, no matter the social situation. From time to time, it also occurred during real estate closings.

Here is an example of his not-so-casual demeanor. We were at a dinner in the city one evening, and regrettably, he was driving. We had parked in a lot in a busy neighborhood, and everyone had left the restaurants in the area simultaneously. We were trying to leave the parking lot, but cars would not allow any vehicle to leave the lot to get onto the street. In utter frustration, my friend's old demons arose, and he swiftly swung the steering wheel and proceeded to drive down the sidewalk to the next street. We were screaming from the back seat as pedestrians were leaping out of the way, dodging our car.

When he became an attorney and fully engaged in his real estate practice, my friend was the most meticulous attorney you could ever imagine. His documentation for every closing was prepared, orderly, correct down to the smallest detail, and accurate beyond criticism. To ensure a smooth closing, whether for the buyer or seller, it was customary for him to deliver the proposed documents to his opponent a week or so before the closing with a cover letter requesting the attorney to review everything and contact him if any modification was needed. There never was.

When circumstances arose, whether spontaneous or contrived, my friend would raise his voice or stand up at the closing table in a threatening manner occasionally to make a point or resolve a sticky issue. This did not occur often, but the real estate community, especially the brokers, loved those shenanigans. Most of the occurrences impressed the clients. All the parties were concerned about was closing the deal to complete the sale so the brokers could receive their commission.

There are hundreds of stories. But one closing was memorable.

A residential real estate deal (I'd had a few) is usually a win-win situation. The seller wants to sell, and the buyer wants to buy the property. For the most part, it's typically non-confrontational. My friend sent out the documents a week before, heard nothing in return, and arrived at the closing ready to close in short order.

It must have been evident to my friend that the opposing attorney had yet to review the closing documents he'd received a week before. The attorney started to leaf through the papers. My friend was angry but, at this point, not hostile. Then the opposing attorney started to mumble something about the documents, either they were not in proper order or some nonsense, and then dared to claim that essential documents were missing or incorrect.

Usually, that would precipitate a brief rebuke and a verbal retort that all the papers were, in fact, correct, accurate, complete, and "If you had read the materials beforehand, you'd be better prepared for this closing." Still, not abusive toward the other attorney but smoldering.

Then, my friend was accused of "not knowing how to handle a real estate closing." That was the last straw.

My friend stood up, forcefully pushed the table with all the documents up against the attorney and his client, and said words to the effect, "Look, you fat f——, one more word out

CONTRITION

of you and I'm going to take you outside and beat the living s—— out of you and your client." Cooler heads calmed the situation down to the extent that they could; the deal was closed, and the opposing attorney was escorted to his car by the brokers in an apoplectic state of shock.

A month or two after that incident, my friend received a complaint from the disciplinary commission filed by the opposing attorney, who'd been threatened, with a word-for-word description of the altercation. The attorney's client may have also endorsed it.

My friend came to my office, visibly disturbed. He'd never been called out for anything, and I mean anything, before.

"What am I supposed to do?" he asked.

I said, "For once in your life, you're going to have to learn a word that has never appeared in your vocabulary —contrition."

"I won't, and I can't," he said. "You're going to have to," I answered.

So, we sat down, and while he was muttering about how he was planning to fulfill his promise about the other attorney, I crafted his "apology" to the disciplinary commission, to the lawyer, and his client, explaining how he "unexpectedly lost self-control" and how his "emotions got the best of his advocacy for his client," He apologized profusely, and, with tongue in cheek, wrote that: "it was the first time he'd ever experienced such uncharacteristic rage at a closing," and how it "will never happen again."

Very reluctantly and with fire in his eyes, he read, signed, and sent the response to everyone involved.

After the response was sent, the disciplinary commission took no action, and, thankfully, the matter was dropped.

Contested Divorce

In the first few years of practice, I handled various disputes, including uncontested and contested divorce matters. The animosity between the parties was usually palpable, and I developed an aversion to handling those cases very early on. I couldn't tolerate the fighting, the lies, the unrealistic demands, and the opposing attorneys. The anger was generated, in large part, by the attorneys who exhibited aggressive behavior to impress their clients.

One such case had nothing to do with the party's positions, and I became involved only by chance.

A friend of mine was having a serious relationship with a woman going through a very hostile, contested divorce. There was a large estate, and the wife was as greedy as one could imagine. Her husband owned a vast, profitable family business, and the wife wanted half of everything in sight. I was only involved in the litigation once my friend was subpoenaed for a deposition with the wife's attorney. He lived in the family home, which incensed the wife, even though she had her residence.

The wife was represented by a seasoned divorce attorney who charged an enormous retainer, and another high-powered divorce attorney represented the husband. The backgrounds of each attorney created an interesting situation. They were lifelong friends. They went to the same high school, played on the same teams, went to college together, were members of the same fraternity, and went to the same law school.

When the deposition began, the two attorneys shot daggers at each other. They were openly hostile to each other, to the extent that whenever a question was asked of my client, it drew an objection. After a short time, the atmosphere in the room got even more heated, and at one point, the husband's attorney yelled "F—— you" at the other attorney, which received a similar loud response. They each stood up threateningly, and if I hadn't intervened, the verbal argument might have deteriorated into an outright fistfight. We terminated the deposition, and it was never reconvened. I couldn't believe the spectacle.

I learned later that they each laughed about the deposition over dinner that night.

No Greek Feast

I needed to familiarize myself with Greek culture. My only contact with anything Greek was a gyro sandwich. So, it was a mystery why a Greek gentleman came to see me about defending a divorce his wife had filed. He had the suit papers with him, and it was a straightforward, boilerplate divorce complaint. The Complaint named all parties, the one minor child, the property they had bought during the short marriage, and her claim for child support, maintenance payments, and a division of personal property. Her first claim was for him to pay her attorney's fees, support money for her housing expenses, and for him to be removed from the marital residence.

We arrived in court for a hearing on the requests, and the wife was present with her attorney. I immediately recognized the central issue in the divorce. My client was close to forty and owned a successful local Greek restaurant. The wife was in her mid-twenties and could have competed in the Ms. Universe contest. She was gorgeous. It soon became apparent that she would have liked to kill me for even speaking with her husband, let alone representing him against her. She shot daggers in my direction every time I spoke.

No Greek Feast

The marital problems stemmed from the age difference and her independence, which he could not tolerate. He was from the old school and expected his wife to be at his beck and call, do housework, and be a mother to their child. She was modern and independent and wanted to be socially active and go out for dinners and dances; he couldn't tolerate that behavior.

Over time, we had to gather all the documents and materials in the marriage, including the residence, who paid for it, what amount, what other assets they had, and proof of his income. He was driving a brand-new luxury automobile and declared a salary from the restaurant of $150 per week. She accused him of conducting his business in cash, hiding assets he owned locally and in Greece, and claiming he was worth substantially more than he would admit.

For as long as the litigation lasted, I started to have anxiety attacks, fearing the staring and outright hostility from the wife. Eventually, the husband relented and agreed to the divorce and reasonable terms for the wife's continuing expenses. I couldn't have been more fearful that she had plans for my demise.

Money

My opinion of divorce practitioners was never high. I never considered that area of the law as something I could do permanently. Most attorneys in that field grasp how the divorce laws apply to the division of property, the care and custody of children, the costs involved in sending children to college, and the provision of funds for housing and support. Occasionally, I've witnessed attorneys aggressively advocate for positions they've created for their clients, even if they were unreasonable.

Several well-known divorce attorneys regularly represented very wealthy couples. They filed and argued documents regularly, arguing for temporary support and attorney's fees from the affluent spouse, asking the judge to evict the spouse, or divulging indiscretions of one of the spouses to curry favor with the judge against the alleged lousy actor.

So, with that background, I found myself sitting in the gallery when two of the most prominent divorce attorneys were arguing before a judge. The wife's attorney was screaming for immediate help for his client. She wanted an immediate trial of the case. The lawyer wished to pay his fees, the wife wanted support money, and the husband was evicted from the residence. One of the children was going to college, and the wife's attorney wanted tuition payments. The lawyer was adamant about a speedy trial that day if the judge could arrange it.

The arguments went on for a long time. The courtroom was packed. Finally, after all the arguments, the judge made some rulings and refused to give the parties the trial the wife so desperately wanted. So, with the arguments ending, the grizzled husband's lawyer started walking out of the courtroom and said, in earshot of the entire audience, "What's her hurry? He owns a dozen fast-food restaurants."

The Eye in the Sky

Whether you know it or not, you're on camera wherever you go, whatever you do, and when you might least expect it. Security cameras are everywhere, and security services watch and tape your activities.

The aisles of a grocery store are being surveilled. A closed-circuit video runs on a city bus, train, or platform twenty-four hours a day. Airports, civic centers, big-box stores, convenience stores, taxicabs, and office buildings are also covered.

Rarely a personal injury event isn't recorded in real-time. Without casting aspersions, I've found that a potential defendant's ability to retrieve a videotape of an incident is not necessarily available or reliable. Policies may be in place that control whether images are retained or when they are scheduled to be destroyed.

If a company's video system has captured pictures of an accident and the company knows a claim may arise from the incident, it may be wrongful to destroy the evidence. In the law, that's known as spoliation of evidence.

It's not uncommon for the photographs to be helpful tothe

defense of a claim; the images are retained longer than if the incident confirms the allegations of the injured claimant. When a person slips, trips, or falls and becomes injured, the injured person's claim must be proven by a preponderance of the evidence. The overriding question is, is the claim being presented more likely valid than not true?

Fall-down cases are challenging. The fact that someone fell and was injured by himself doesn't prove the property owner was negligent or at fault for causing the incident or injuries. A person claiming they lost as a result of a property owner's negligence has the burden of proving the owner or manager either created the problem, like allowing a broken downspout to leak on a sidewalk and freeze, or knew the defect existed for a sufficient amount of time to correct it but ignored the problem.

The injured person has a different burden. If the problem was observed and they fell, they might be more guilty than the owner. In Illinois, if the injured person is more than 50 percent responsible for the event, they are barred from collecting.

An additional defense that the property owner may raise is that if the defect was open and obvious, the injured person should have avoided it. Or if the defect is so insignificant, it may be unactionable, as a de minimis defect, with no recovery. There are numerous other obstacles to recovery. A person is required to keep a lookout for hazards. Most incidents raise questions about the injured person noticing the problem or notifying the owner in adequate time to allow them to correct the defect. Many fall-down claims are defeated through the claimant's mouth when asked, "Did you see the defect before you tripped and fell?" It is rare when a person admits they saw it but fell anyway. Then, the defense points to the claimant's negligence, in not being attentive, as the cause of the fall.

To complicate matters further, there's the deliberate encounter or unavoidable hazard where the injured person had no other means of avoiding the risk. In those cases, a jury compares the two competing arguments and usually deducts a percentage of fault, up to 50 percent, which is deducted from any award.

The deliberate encounter was at the crux of a case involving one of my clients. He was a frequent vendor in an indoor farmers' market. The venue was a large open barn-like structure, allowing vendors to display their goods on tables in numbered booths. There were dozens of vendors. The building had one large open doorway, with an overhead door through which the vendors had to bring their flatbeds and carts of merchandise. At either side of the doorway was a patio with tables and benches for outside seating for attendees arriving early to gain admittance right at the opening.

All vendors were required to enter the venue at a specific time, well before the day's event. As one might imagine, many of them showed up around the same time and clogged the entryway with their vehicles and carts. It had been freezing on the day of the incident with my client, and the patio areas were caked with ice.

My client couldn't park his vehicle near the entry door and had to park on the nearby access road adjacent to the building along a fence separating the street from the patio areas. He had unloaded his merchandise, placed it in his booth, and was walking out of the building to move his vehicle, but parked cars near the door blocked his path, so he stepped onto the patio area to reach his vehicle. The patio was caked with black ice, and as he stepped into the patio area, his feet slipped on the ice, and he struck his head, rendering him unconscious with a severe head injury.

Our leading theory in presenting the case centered on the fact that because his path was blocked, preventing him from walking on the driveway leading to the building's doorway, he had no alternative exit but to walk on the patio area and encounter the slippery patio. Added to that was the negligence

The Eye in the Sky

of the farmers' market organizer, who arranged to spread ice-melting chemicals on the driveway and not on the patio, where it would have been reasonable for vendors to walk to get to their vehicles.

One aspect of slip-and-fall occurrences involves the actions of the premises owner or manager. If ice forms naturally, other than from a leaking gutter or downspout, and a landowner does nothing to correct it, it is regarded as "natural accumulation" and not actionable. Once a person voluntarily undertakes to remedy the natural accumulation of snow or ice, they must do so in a non-negligent manner.

After several depositions, we proved that the organizer voluntarily sought to take measures for ice removal, focusing only on their profit-making enterprise and not being concerned about the vendors' and visitors' safety.

Given the circumstances, it was plausible that vendors and customers of the farmers' market would walk in the open area of the patios and encounter the icy walkways. We also proved that our clients needed to be more focused while walking out of the venue, avoiding the hustle and bustle of the other vendors' activities and moving their merchandise into the building. The claim was settled before trial, a rare outcome for slip-and-fall cases in that jurisdiction.

The Tables Were Turned

There was an occasion years ago when I represented a man who fell on an icy stoop immediately outside the front door of his rental apartment building. The janitor had tried to plow snow from the stoop, which led to a short-paved walkway connected to the parking lot where his car was parked. He was exiting the front door. His foot landed on a patch of ice on the stoop, and he fell, fracturing his ankle.

We filed suit claiming the attempt at ice and snow removal was negligent and completed all the written discovery. At my client's deposition, he identified photographs he took of the doorway, the stoop, the piles of snow and ice, and the walkway to the parking lot. The walkway from the snow-covered stoop to the parking lot was separate from the city sidewalk.

At the time, local city ordinances required property owners to clear their walkways and sidewalks adjacent to the property.

After all the written discovery was completed and my client and the janitor had been deposed, the defendant's attorney prepared and filed a document requesting the judge to enter summary judgment in favor of the landlord.

A summary judgment motion presents the argument

The Tables Were Turned

thatno facts in controversy need to be decided, and the moving party is entitled to judgment as a matter of law. It defeats the case in its entirety.

The judge heard arguments on the motion and decided that the stoop and walkway were sufficiently considered part of the city sidewalk, even though they were not connected to it, and he entered summary judgment. It was a bitter defeat with which I strongly disagreed. I advised the client of the judge's ruling, and we appealed the decision. The appellate court agreed with the judge's order, and our case ended.

The rest of the story was worse if that wasn't a bitter enough ending. I had a close relative who was a defense attorney. Unbeknownst to me, he was handling a fall-down case on snow and ice, which involved a fact pattern like the case I lost. Out of the clear blue sky, he phoned me one day with the news that he had just won a summary judgment motion, and he cited my case as the legal authority that gave him the win. Ouch.

What Happened?

Even the most seasoned attorneys can lose their concentration, and I witnessed such a blunder, not just from one attorney but two simultaneously, during the same deposition. My client had tripped and fallen on an icy sidewalk in the common areas of a condominium townhome property. The ice had formed from a dripping downspout from one unit and spread over the sidewalk. The sidewalk had places where the sidewalk panels had settled unevenly, and the water leaking from the downspout collected near the cracks, which created a slipping hazard. Snowfall during the night obscured the icy area. When my client left his residence to walk to his vehicle parked at the rear of the property, he slipped and fell, fracturing his leg. He was transported to a local hospital, where surgery had to be performed. Pins and screws were used to reassemble his femur, the long bone in his leg.

We filed suit against the owner of the townhome, which had the leaky downspout, and the snow removal/plowing company for not clearing the snow. Two separate insurance carriers were involved, and each retained different defense firms. The assigned attorneys blamed the other for causing the unnatural accumulation of ice and claimed it was the plaintiff's fault for not seeing the icy formation. If they proved my client was more than 50 percent at fault for his injury, he would be barred from collecting any damages.

The plaintiff's deposition was scheduled, which would allow both defense attorneys the right to question the plaintiff. Both showed up with lengthy outlines of questions. The court rules allowed depositions to be conducted within three hours unless a judge extended the time. Realizing that slips and falls on icy walks were some of the most contested types of cases, I was careful to prepare my client for any questions that might be asked. The defenses to those types of cases are numerous and devastating. Defenses focus on any number of issues. The plaintiff's failure to keep a proper lookout for problems, lack of notice to the landowner in sufficient time to correct the defect, and open and obvious hazards that the plaintiff failed to see are often fatal to a claim.

We arrived at the defense counsel's office, and the questioning began. They asked all the preliminary questions, including his education, going back to high school, and his work history and they even went into his marital status. He'd been divorced. Questions were asked about his residences over the past twenty years when he bought his first house, what he knew about ordinances requiring homeowners to clear sidewalks of snow and ice, and if he had used ice-melting chemicals in the past. They asked where he would purchase shovels and chemicals.

Then, they asked about how it came to be that he bought the townhouse where the fall occurred. This property had eight townhouses, so they asked questions about each owner, how long they lived there, if he knew them socially if they cleared their walkways during winter, and how it was done. They inquired about the parking lot at the rear of the property and how the spaces were assigned. Then they showed him photographs of the property, with images of each townhouse, each parking space, the sidewalk at the property, and how each townhouse owner had personalized the front of their unit.

Then, the questioning turned to the injuries. My client testified that when the fall occurred, one of the neighbors called the police, and the police summoned the paramedic ambulance. They asked about the immediate care of the paramedics, how they stabilized the fracture, placed him on a gurney, and took him to the emergency department of a nearby hospital. That hospital didn't have an orthopedic surgeon on call, so my client was taken to another hospital, where he was evaluated and admitted for surgery. My client's leg was so swollen the surgery had to be scheduled when the swelling subsided, so he was an inpatient for three or four days before the surgery. The attorneys inquired about each day spent in the hospital. Then, he was asked about how he was taken to a rehabilitation facility for healing and, later, for intense physical and occupational therapy.

He was then asked how he had progressed and what his daily activities had been since his discharge from care. The details of which lasted a long, long time. The questioning had already taken two hours and forty-five minutes, and I reminded the defense counsel that at the three-hour mark, by rule, the deposition would be concluded, and we were leaving. They were still questioning my client about his current activities of daily life when they hit the three-hour mark, never asking him one question about how his fall occurred. They made a weak objection to our leaving. At that point, I reminded them of the deposition time-limit rule again.

I told them that if they had budgeted their time more efficiently and had not been so curious about irrelevant matters, they would have had sufficient time to inquire about all the pertinent issues in the case. I was confident and comfortable taking the action that I did, knowing that even if the defense attorneys sought to present a motion to the judge,

What Happened?

asking him to allow them to reconvene the deposition to ask the pertinent questions they might have needed to establish how the incident occurred, no judge would accept the argument that they needed more than the three hours they wasted to depose my client regarding a fall down on an icy sidewalk. I thanked the defense counsel for their time and effort, told my client we were leaving, and we departed.

In the elevator, my client asked me, "What just happened?"

I told him about the three-hour rule and how the defense attorneys were so involved in asking questions on their prepared outline that they lost track of time, asked wholly irrelevant lines of questions, and broke the rule, which allowed us to terminate the deposition and leave. "Could you do that?" he asked.

"We just did," I responded.

Shortly after that deposition, they called me to discuss a global settlement, each contributing a portion. After further negotiations and discussing the risks and benefits of a compromise, he accepted the offer, and we resolved the case.

Safety Last

It's no secret that if you want to accomplish anything, don't organize a committee or involve a government entity. Whether it's endemic to the system or not, the goal of conceiving, planning, getting funding, and starting a project of any size can encounter delays. When a government entity is involved, the approval process can cause the project cost to increase beyond the expectation of the bidding contractors.

So, with those basic understandings, a horrible accident occurred involving a client's husband, who was killed in a trench collapse on a government sewer project. The entity that planned and issued bid invitations was a park district in a wealthy suburb. The bidding process was completed, but the issuance of permits was delayed for months. By the time the permits were issued to begin the work, the low bidder, the sewer contractor, was losing money to the extent that they were barely breaking even. Government contracts are awarded to the lowest bidder, so any profit margin would already be thin.

In sewer construction, trenches are often dug to complete the work. Many federal and state safety regulations control that type of workplace. If a trench is dug below grade a certain distance, devices must be placed along the walls, either shoring or a steel brace, commonly known as a sandbox, lowered into the excavation. Those are placed in the trench to hold back both sides of the walls and protect workers from collapse.

My client's husband was a young Hispanic man working as a "bottom man." After the trench was dug, the bottom workers would lower the sewer pipe sections with a crane, and the "bottom man," using his hands and levers, would join the sewer sections together.

After the sewer pipes were laid, more trenching was done to extend the lines to the length necessary to hook them up to the main structure. After completing the project, the shoring or sandbox would be removed, and the trenches would be backfilled to ground level.

In this particular job, there were time delays between the bidding process, the contract signing, and the job's start. Unfortunately, due to the time delays, the contractor started to cut corners, and the project faced rising costs. The most dangerous thing they did, which led to the tragic accident that eventually killed my client's husband, was the failure to use shoring or a sandbox. The contractor was "bird-dogging" the job to finish as quickly as possible to salvage some profit from the contract. They failed to place shoring or a sandbox in the excavation.

After we filed suit and engaged in discovery, the postmortem investigation revealed that the ground on the side of the trench was 27 percent sand, which was very unstable. As they dug, the trench walls collapsed onto my client's husband and caused his death. It was a gruesome death being buried alive. He left his surviving wife and two children under the age of five.

I immediately prepared and filed a lawsuit, which had to

be filed in a county known for its affluence and conservative population. It had a tiny Hispanic community.

At the very outset of the case, the defense inundated me with discovery requests, motions presented to the judge for enforcement of discovery, and countless attempts to dismiss my client's case. They were filing documents that required my appearance.

I was not a county resident, which the defense made abundantly clear to the judge every time we stepped into the courtroom. After months of those tactics, with my client's consent, we contacted a local, experienced trial attorney to assist me. The waters settled down once he entered his appearance, and the harassment ended. He was well known to the defense attorneys and from their county, and they had immense respect for him.

We conducted dozens of depositions and exchanged many documents, which gave us insight into what had occurred. The contractor was grossly negligent in not providing the safety devices necessary to protect the workers in the trenches. We made several attempts to resolve the case, which we estimated had a verdict value of millions of dollars. The deceased was a young man, about twenty-five years of age, earning approximately $40,000 a year.

He left a grieving widow and two very young children. She wasn't able to work and was not fluent in English. She had to testify through an interpreter.

It's hard to express grief through that process. But that was our client, and as a trial lawyer, you must deal with reality.

The defense resisted every suggestion we had toward settlement discussions. So, a jury trial was scheduled.

Every jury trial begins with the selection of the jury. The assigned judge calls for a pool of jurors who will be questioned and qualified to sit as impartial judges of the facts. Each litigant is usually allowed to ask the potential jurors and analyze their ability to be fair and unbiased. The litigants may face challenges if they feel a potential juror cannot be fair.

One of the goals of any litigant's counsel is to avoid selecting a juror who may be so forceful and persuasive that he or she would constitute a one-person jury, directing the remainder of the jury to vote as he or she directs.

Professionals, engineers, and executives are typically excluded because of their leadership skills and power of persuasion. Litigants want every juror to state their opinions and vote as they understand the evidence. The litigants are only granted a certain number of peremptory challenges.

In my local jurisdiction, the pool of jurors is usually made up of middle-class families, workers, tradesmen, and teachers. A person with an advanced degree seldom appears in a jury pool. Unfortunately, in my jurisdiction, people did not honor their commitment and civil responsibility to serve on juries. Everyone summoned would come to serve in the county where our case was being tried. I needed to prepare for the pool of jurors in the courtroom.

When the jurors are summoned to court, they usually complete a short questionnaire with personal questions about their identity, age, address, occupation, and other personal information. Juries are typically composed of twelve jurors, and a pool of thirty-six is usually called to a courtroom. The presiding judge usually asks preliminary questions of the entire pool: Is anyone currently engaged in litigation? Does anyone have family members who are policemen, firemen, or attorneys? Does anyone know any of the parties? There's usually a list of witnesses given to the judge, and they would ask if any potential juror knew any of them. They may be asked if they are parties to a pending lawsuit. If they answer in the affirmative, the judge can excuse them "for cause," and they are dismissed from service in that case.

Once the preliminary questions have been asked of the pool, the clerk of court calls twelve names, and the jury box is filled. The jurors are questioned in panels of four. The judge then may ask those seated some additional questions. Then, he'll turn over the first panel of jurors to the plaintiff's counsel, us.

The first panel consisted of an accountant, an engineer, a teacher, and a retired executive for a multinational corporation. The four members were then questioned more extensively. My colleague handed me the juror questionnaires to review. As soon as I read the cards, beads of sweat started pouring out of every pore in my body.

I asked my counsel, "How can we use our five preemptory challenges on the first four jurors?"

He casually responded, "Relax, these are the good ones." I choked back tears.

We eventually agreed on an entire panel of jurors, and the case began in earnest. We organized and planned the trial in two sections. First, we had the police officers who responded to the scene. Then, we called the emergency paramedics, who retrieved the body. They gave vivid testimony of how they finally located the body and how the deceased was impaled on the leveling pipe and crushed by the collapse.

We presented the coroner to prove the collapse caused the worker's death. We also presented the supervisors and workers, who admitted they didn't use shoring or a sandbox, and we established the ground's sand content.

Then, we had to present the widow, who testified haltingly, even through the interpretation. She discussed their lives, their children's birth, their late father's devotion, and how dynamic he was as a sewer worker.

Finally, we presented a retained expert economist who calculated our client's husband's current and future earnings and estimated the family's economic loss at approximately $600,000.

The evidence went in flawlessly. Every witness testified honestly, forthrightly, and convincingly. Our plan for the case

Safety Last

worked efficiently, and after the next three days, we rested. The defense couldn't have been more substantial and more persuasive. Their only focus was on the testimony of our economist, who was a well-known economics professor at a nearby college with vast testifying experience. He brought our PowerPoint presentations and charts on the growth of wages. He testified convincingly of the lost wages my client's husband would have earned for his expected life span. It totaled well over $600,000. The defense rested.

After the closing of all the evidence, the judge reads specific jury instructions on the law. The cardinal rule is that the jury is instructed to analyze the evidence from the witnesses and apply the law, which is read to the jury by the judge. Exhibits are gathered and given to the jury, and the twelve jurors are escorted to an anteroom to deliberate. They are not to be disturbed until they reach a verdict.

The jury retired to deliberate, and the counsel for all sides shook hands, wished each other success, and parted ways to await the verdict. The case was tried very professionally, and each side was satisfied with their presentations.

Hours went by. At five o'clock, the judge called in the jury and asked if they'd reached a verdict. They answered no but thought they were progressing, so they asked to reconvene the next day. The next day came and went, and after eight more hours, the jurors said they were getting closer and requested one more day to iron out some issues. Finally, on the third day, the jury announced they had reached a unanimous verdict. We were called to the courthouse, and the jury gave their verdict after everyone appeared. The verdict favored the widow, and the amount of the judgment was the amount of the decedent's lost wages.

We were shocked and dismayed. The judge polled the jury, asking each juror if the verdict was their decision, and each said yes. The judge entered judgment on the verdict, and the jury was discharged. We explained the verdict to the widow and left.

It was common for jurors to stand around and discuss aspects of the trial with counsel for either side. In this case, one of the jurors pulled us aside, and we could sense she wasn't entirely satisfied with the outcome.

The juror explained what had happened during the deliberations. Three jurors voted for the plaintiff and wanted to issue a $2 million verdict. Six jurors wanted to award the lost wage amount. The remaining jurors didn't want to enter any verdict for the plaintiff for the express, bigoted reason that they wouldn't reward the Hispanic wife who "didn't testify in English." They wouldn't award $2 million for "any Mexican in this county."

The three-day deliberation was due to the jurors' intimidation by the bloc of six who wouldn't budge on the verdict for the lost wages.

We asked if the juror would sign an affidavit but couldn't convince her to do so. We were stuck with the prejudice-fueled verdict.

I was despondent and never recovered from that outright bigotry. After that, I tried to resolve any cases I had in that county without proceeding to a full-blown jury trial. It was a bitter lesson, one which I never forgot.

Verdict Against the Passive Defendant

One of my first jury trials was memorable only because after the trial and the verdict was returned in our favor, the insurance company's claim representative came to our office to meet the rookie trial attorney who obtained the verdict.

I learned that insurance carriers monitor law firms and keep records of attorneys who try cases and those who refuse to go to court and permanently settle.

They keep track of the doctors who testify, the clinics that treat injured plaintiffs, and the settlement amounts. Everything is in a database that all insurance carriers use as resources. The case I tried and "won" had a simple fact pattern.

A vehicle was traveling north on a busy road in one of the northern suburbs. The road was four lanes wide. There was a side street, which formed a T with the northbound highway. Vehicles exiting from the side street would have to turn left (south) or right when they came to the intersection.

A vehicle exiting from the east onto the road made a left-hand turn when my client's northbound vehicle struck it. My firm represented the northbound vehicle and had already collected damages from the striking vehicle's carrier.

At the time of the collision, a car carrier had been parked on the east side of the roadway, just south of the intersection, and the defendant in the striking vehicle testified that the truck obstructed her view so she could not see the northbound vehicle before she pulled out into the intersection.

The truck's insurance carrier refused to participate in settlement discussions, so we proceeded with the jury trial against the truck's carrier.

During discovery, I obtained photographs of the intersection, which revealed no parking signs along each side of the roadway. This established that the truck was illegally parked when the collision occurred.

We presented all the evidence before a jury and the witnesses, including the truck driver, the at-fault car driver, and my northbound client. The jury deliberated for three hours and returned a verdict in our favor against the truck's insurance carrier. However, the verdict was less than what we had already collected from the first striking vehicle, so we had no new money. However, we obtained a judgment against a passive vehicle. We impressed the truck's insurance adjuster, who wanted to meet me to determine how a new attorney could have accomplished that result.

No Pain, No Suffering, No Recovery, No Leg

Statistics indicate that claims for professional negligence are the most difficult to prove. The ratio in Cook County has been estimated to be 80 percent not guilty. The percentages are much higher in suburban counties outside of Cook County.

A prominent, nationally known trial attorney was trying a case against a surgeon who had amputated a woman's leg. The wrong leg. A lawsuit for medical negligence had to be filed in a western suburban court. By the time the discovery had been completed, with expert witnesses on both sides of the issue, it was clear that the surgeon had not conformed to the standard of care of other surgeons, and the woman's leg was amputated in error.

The plaintiff testified about her visits to the surgeon and her loss, how she had to adapt her daily life activities, fitting prosthetics to the leg, and her inability to do things she enjoyed prior to her surgical accident. A " day in the life" video was played for the jury, showing dramatically how she managed with the artificial leg from when she awoke to her bedtime routine. It covered her house, driving a vehicle, shopping, and recreational activities.

When a medical negligence case is presented, the plaintiff must plead and prove that the defendant physician, surgeon, or practitioner's care and treatment fell below an acceptable standard of care. That opinion must be presented by a physician who practices in the same field of medicine. The proof must convince a jury that the position of the testifying physician or surgeon is more probably true than not true. Many physicians refuse to testify against another physician.

Physicians accused of medical negligence and their insurance carriers have many resources available to defend medical malpractice claims. In this case, the plaintiff's expert, the plaintiff, and the defendant agreed that the accused surgeon had committed negligent care, and the loss of the woman's leg was directly attributable to that negligence.

When the evidence had concluded, the judge read the jury instructions on the law and specific documents that had been admitted into evidence. Those were submitted to the jury for their deliberations. The plaintiff and counsel were confident that a verdict in her favor would be entered. The defendant's counsel had argued against a high verdict, claiming that any verdict should be fair and reasonable despite the strong evidence against his client.

A few hours after deliberations began, the jury signaled to the judge that they had reached a verdict, and the parties and their attorneys gathered in the courtroom. The jury was allowed to enter the courtroom, and the judge inquired if they had reached a verdict.

"We have," answered the foreperson.

"Would you hand the verdict form to the clerk," said the judge.

The verdict form was handed to the clerk, and the judge ordered the clerk to read the verdict. The foreperson read,

"We, the duly impaneled jury in the above matter, find the defendant not guilty." The attorneys all gasped, as did the plaintiff.

No Pain, No Suffering, No Recovery, No Leg

The judge polled the jury, and they all responded that the verdict was correct. Curiously, many of the jurors remained in the courtroom after the verdict was read, and the obvious question was, "How did they reach that decision?"

"Well," one juror said, "we listened to all of the testimony and the evidence and watched the video of her, and we all figured she's getting around okay with the prosthetic." There was no sympathy, compassion, pain or suffering, loss of earnings, or recovery. Even the judge was surprised at the outcome.

The moral of the story is that some jurisdictions have jurors who are immune to claims for personal injury cases and will not consider the elements of proven negligence or damages despite the evidence.

Hostile Work Environment

One of the saddest cases I was ever asked to handle was the result of a delusional man who had imagined a budding relationship between him and a female coworker in his department. The man was infatuated with this young girl half his age, who, by all accounts, was a sweet, friendly, enthusiastic, kind, and beautiful person. She was pleasant to everyone. The man completely misinterpreted her demeanor as provocative to him. He contrived in his twisted mind that they had a relationship. That was not the case.

He approached her with infatuation at some point, and she emphatically rebuffed him. His mind must have snapped. Within a few weeks after their "confrontation," he plotted his revenge. One morning, he called in sick and told his supervisor that he would not be in the office that day. He drove to the secure parking facility for their company and parked his vehicle next to hers. He waited until she left work that day and confronted her in the parking lot. When she resisted his assault against her, he stabbed her multiple times and killed her. He left the parking lot and drove home. A few hours later, when her body was discovered, the police investigators reviewed the security video from the parking lot and found his vehicle entering the lot, parking next to her car, the assault against her, and his departure.

The assailant knew there was video surveillance in the parking lot. He knew he had to use his pass card to enter the lot. He also knew that all the staircases were equipped with video cameras. When the police viewed the videotape evidence, his arrest was immediate.

The prosecution of his criminal case was conclusive as to his guilt, and since he was about to be found guilty of the murder, facing the death penalty, he pleaded guilty with no provision for parole. Due to the brutality of the crime, the judge added the stipulation that if the man ever sought to review the decision or the sentence, the guilty verdict and the death penalty would be reinstated. My task was to determine whether this crime could have been avoided and if the employer and manager of the building had any liability exposure for inadequate security.

During our discovery, the state's attorney produced a copy of the autopsy, which included photographs of the girl's body, which was the first time I had ever been exposed to such gruesome images. It motivated me to search every possible avenue of liability against the building owner and manager.

I was motivated to look under every rock. My discovery was expansive. My first request was for the murderer's employee folder. I discovered numerous complaints from the deceased girl about his sexual harassment of her, as well as complaints from other female employees. There were disciplinary letters from the company about those episodes and suspension letters with warnings about his behavior. Some of the comments accused the murderer of creating a hostile work environment, which proved the employer had actual notice of his bad behavior.

The building management company was accused of inadequate security. I found the security service's staffing records. Other than placing cameras at the parking lot and entry points to the building, no live person monitored the cameras, and the security company records revealed they needed help hiring individuals to be stationed in the security office.

When I achieved a settlement of the claims, the family was eternally grateful for recovery and for bringing closure to a horrible episode in their lives—the loss of a dear sister and daughter whose life should have been protected.

Conclusion

The following hangs framed in the lobby of Northwestern University Law School. Students pass it daily while going to and from their classes. I would
like to share the words of Louis Lande, written in a dedication to the new home for the New York County Lawyers' Association in New York City.

I Am the Lawyer
Louis Lande
I am the Lawyer.
I displaced brute force with Mercy, Justice and Equity.
I taught Mankind to respect the rights of others to their property, to their personal liberty, to freedom of conscience, to free speech and free assembly.
I am the spokesman of every righteous cause.
I plead for the poor, the persecuted, the widow and the orphan.
I maintain honor in the market place.
I am the champion of unpopular causes.
I am the foe of tyranny, oppression and bureaucracy.

Conclusion

I prepared the way for the Ten Commandments.
I pleaded for the freedom of the slave in Greece and for the captive in Rome.
I fought the Stamp Act.
I wrote the Declaration of Independence and the Rights of Man.
I defended the Slave. I was an abolitionist. I signed the Emancipation Proclamation.
In every land and in every clime,
I punish the wicked, protect the innocent, raise up the lowly, oppose brutality and injustice.
I fought in every war for Liberty.
I stand in the way of public clamor and the tyranny of the majority.
I speak for the rich man when prejudice prevents him from getting justice, and
I insist that the poor man be accorded all his rights and privileges.
I seek the equality of mankind, regardless of color, caste, sex or religion.
I am for the Parliament of Man and for the abolition of all Wars.
I hate fraud, deceit and trickery.
I am forbidden to serve two masters or to compromise with injustice.
I am the conservative of the past, the liberal of the present, and the radical of the future.
I believe in convention, but I cut the Gordian Knot of formalism and red tape to do Justice and Equity.
I am the leader of mankind in every crisis.
I am the scapegoat of the World.
I hold the rights of Mankind in the hollow of my hand, but am unable to obtain recognition of my own.
I am the pioneer, but I am the last to reverence the past and to overturn the present.

Conclusion

I am the just judge and the righteous ruler.
I hear before I condemn.
I seek the best in everything.

About the Author

Leo Bleiman is a native of Chicago, growing up in the neighborhood of Albany Park, at the end of the Ravenswood elevated train line. He attended Hibbard Elementary School and Theodore Roosevelt High School, graduating in 1961. His educational journey was unremarkable, unless you consider being labeled as the "class clown" in high school. He had wonderful, inspiring and high achieving classmates and friends who formed the social athletic club, known as the Torpedoes, who took him under their wing, and encouraged him to attend college, instead of working in a family business. His family started and ran a company which employed blind and handicapped individuals, sewing household goods and weaving rag rugs. Working alongside his Mother and Father, brothers, Ted (of blessed memory) Jay and sister Susan, Leo learned the value of hard work.

He finally honed his study skills and received a Bachelor

of Arts degree in English from Roosevelt University, where his instructors and professors imbued him with an appreciation of literature and writing. After graduation from Roosevelt, he became an elementary school instructor for a short period of time, where he met his life partner, Jill. Eventually, Leo enrolled in Chicago Kent College of Law, becoming licensed to practice in May, 1972. Upon being licensed he entered a general practice, handling nearly every imaginable type of case, from real estate closings, evictions, commercial collection cases and divorces. His most satisfying work was from personal injury cases and work injury claims.

He credits his wife, Jill, whose constant support, encouragement and interest in the cases he handled led him to recall and draft summaries of some of the most interesting and challenging cases he's handled in his fifty (50) years of practice. Aside from Jill, Leo has been blessed with two sons, two daughters-in-law, six grandchildren and a circle of friends, family and colleagues who have enriched his life and led him to compose this reminiscence. He continues to practice and contribute his experiences and the practical aspects of practicing law with younger attorneys.